B
7:
AI

Genesis 1-11

FOUNDATIONS OF REALITY

CWR

Jeremy Thomson

Contents

Introduction

The early chapters of Genesis are of great importance for understanding the whole Bible. They set the stage on which the subsequent drama of redemption takes place, first in the story of Israel, and second in the story of the Church that is born out of the passion of Israel's Messiah. The final chapters of Revelation return to important themes that are set out here at the beginning.

However, for over a century these chapters have generated more controversy than any other part of the Bible. Since the publication of Darwin's *On the Origin of Species by Means of Natural Selection* (1859), the theory of evolution has become the established scientific orthodoxy, and some have argued from it against belief in a divine creator. Christians are united in resisting that conclusion, since God's creative work underlies everything else in the Bible, especially the work of Jesus Christ. Yet the theory of evolution does not in itself rule out belief in a divine creator; indeed many Christians think that it provides scientific insight into the process of creation.

These studies advocate neither the theory of evolution nor its alternative, known as 'creation science'. The claim that God created the world is a matter of faith, grounded in God's self-revelation (Heb. 11:3). The opening chapters of Genesis are thus a confession of faith, rather than a collection of independently verifiable accounts of world origins. Having said this, the biblical writers made use of knowledge of the natural world that was available to them in their culture to shape the content of their witness to God's creative activity. Israel's thinkers asked *how* questions about creation, as well as *who* and *why* questions. Thus our interpretation of Genesis will be aided by modern discoveries about their ancient culture.

Although Moses has traditionally been associated with Genesis, along with Exodus to Deuteronomy, at least some of the material postdates him (eg the expression 'of the Chaldeans', Gen. 11:28,31, belongs to the first millennium BC). We cannot know who the final author was, though there is much to be said for the view that ancient oral and written traditions were incorporated into the book familiar to us at the height of the Babylonian Empire (prior to or during the captivity in Babylon, 596–538 BC). The Jews were then under great cultural inducement to adopt Babylonian religion and its world-view. A Christian reading of these chapters will be alert to equivalent cultural inducements of contemporary 'empires'.

The first 11 chapters of Genesis should be understood in relation to the whole book. One indication of this is a literary structuring device. The Hebrew word *toledoth* is translated 'account' in the NIV, but a better translation is 'generations' or 'family history'. The noun *toledoth* comes from the verb *yalad*, 'to bear, give birth', and fruitfulness expresses the central theme of the whole book from creation (1:28) to the overcoming of infertility and famine in the patriarchal stories. Now *toledoth* appears at the head of ten main sections of Genesis: 2:4; 5:1; 6:9; 10:1; 11:10; 11:27; 25:12; 25:19; 36:1 (repeated at 36:9); 37:2. The hymn-like creation account (1:1–2:3) forms a distinct prologue to the whole book, followed by ten sections, five before Abraham and five concerning Abraham and his descendants.

The right-hand side of Table I.1 shows there is some symmetry between the five primeval sections and the five patriarchal sections (though they are of unequal length). The central story in each 'half' turns on the expression 'God remembered Noah/Rachel' (8:1; 30:22); the salvation of the human race (and the animals) from the Flood finds a parallel in the remedy for the barrenness of Jacob's beloved wife in the key section recounting the birth of his sons, ancestors of the twelve tribes of Israel. These two central stories are each surrounded by genealogies, and then by outer passages that tie the two halves together:

Table I.1 The literary structure of the book of Genesis

1:1–2:3	*Creation Hymn*	Prologue
2:4–4:26	*Account of heavens and earth*	Adam & Eve; Cain & Abel; genealogy
5:1–6:8	*Account of Adam*	Genealogy; the sons of God
6:9–9:29	*Account of Noah*	**The Flood story**
10:1–11:9	*Account of Noah's sons*	Genealogy; Tower of Babel
11:10–26	*Account of Shem*	Genealogy – Shem to Abram
11:27–25:11	*Account of Terah*	Abraham stories
25:12–18	*Account of Ishmael*	Genealogy
25:19–35:29	*Account of Isaac*	**Jacob – 12 sons**
36:1–37:1	*Account of Esau*	Genealogy
37:2–50:26	*Account of Jacob*	Joseph stories

- The Abraham stories are introduced by the genealogy of Shem.
- The Joseph stories come to a theological conclusion in Joseph's statement to his brothers, 'Am I in the place of God?' (50:19), that begins to answer the serpent's original temptation, 'You will be like God' (3:5).

The prologue thus stands apart somewhat from the Adam and Eve story and sets the scene for both the primeval stories and the patriarchal stories. These two 'halves' of the book are interdependent; the primeval stories set the scene for the origins of God's chosen people, and they remind readers of Israel's story that its calling was always intended to bring blessing to 'all peoples on earth' (12:3).

These first chapters of the Bible may be said to lay the foundations of reality. They train our thinking to adjust to God's perspective on all that exists. They diagnose central problems in human relationships and begin to reveal God's character in His response to them.

WEEK ONE

Creation

Opening Icebreaker

Have any people in the group encountered 'culture shock' when visiting a foreign country, or meeting people from a very different racial or age background. What misunderstandings or mistakes were made? What have people learned about cultural differences?

Bible Reading

- Genesis 1:1–2:3

Opening our Eyes

This passage forms the prologue to the whole book of Genesis. It is not really poetry, but its highly patterned use of language gives it a solemn, hymn-like quality. There are many repetitions of key phrases and words, though without adherence to rigid formulae:

- × 10: 'God said', 'let' (as a command), 'God... made', 'according to their kind';
- × 7: 'and there/it was so', 'and God saw that it was (very) good';
- × 3: 'God called', 'God blessed', 'God created', 'God created man (and woman)';
- 3 × 7: 'earth/ground/land'.

There is also a strong literary structure: the first three days concern three realm-separations, and the second group of three days concerns what fills the realms so established. Both Day 3 and Day 6 have double acts of creation, so that there are eight acts of creation in all. Thus Days 4 to 6 form a parallel panel with Days 1 to 3. The completion on Day 7 echoes the preparation (Table 1.1).

Table 1.1 Literary structure of Genesis 1:1–23

Preparation (1:1–2) [formless and empty]	
A. Separations forming static regions	**B. Filling with mobile occupants**
Day 1 (1:3–5) light/darkness (day/night)	**Day 4 (1:14–19)** luminaries
Day 2 (1:6–8) water/expanse/water (sky)	**Day 5 (1:20–23)** fish and birds
Day 3 (1:9–13) water/dry ground (land/seas) vegetation	**Day 6 (1:24–31)** animals humans
Day 7 (2:1–3) – Completion ['the heavens and the earth... and... all their vast array']	

Archaeologists have discovered a number of early stories of origins from the Ancient Near East: the *Enuma Elish*, the *Atrahasis Epic*, the *Gilgamesh Epic*. Such writings have some historical features – an interest in past people and events – and thus do not float outside time like fairy stories. Yet they also seem to portray things somewhat 'larger than life' and thus have been labelled 'epics'. When these writings are compared with Genesis 1–11, it seems likely that Genesis was written in response to such stories of origins. Although Genesis 1–11 shares certain assumptions with these epics (eg there is an invisible supernatural world), it differs from them in significant ways. In particular, certain polemical points are made in Genesis 1, providing an alternative world-view to those generally accepted in the Ancient Near East:

- The sun and moon are not named; they are simply called 'lights' (vv14–18). The stars appear almost as an afterthought. These luminaries are not deities, as they often were in ancient polytheism, nor do they rule human life.
- The unusual verb 'create' is used at the start (1:1) and at the conclusion (2:3) as well as at the climax three times (v27), but it is also used at verse 21. Here it counters taking sea monsters as gods, as they often were in the ancient world.
- In the *Enuma Elish* (the Babylonian creation story), there is a battle among the gods, won by Marduk who creates heaven and earth from the body of the slain female god, Tiamat. In Genesis, God creates, having uttered His word, and so communication rather than violence is built into the very fabric of creation.
- In several of the ancient stories, humans are made to be servants of the gods. In Genesis humans are the climax of creation, and given responsibility for the rest of the world.
- Egyptian and Mesopotamian cultures understood the role of imaging God as belonging to the king. Here in Genesis the monarchical office is 'democratised', because all human beings are royal images of God.

Discussion Starters

1. What strikes you about the way in which God sets off creation in this whole passage?

_____

_____

_____

_____

2. Subsequent chapters will introduce a much more ambiguous understanding of the world, but how is the creation evaluated here, and what attitude to the world does this commend?

_____

_____

_____

_____

3. What sort of God do we meet in this passage?

_____

_____

_____

_____

4. What does it mean to say that human beings are created in God's image (1:27)? Look at the immediate context for clues.

_____

_____

_____

_____

5. In modern Western politics (since the eighteenth century), human beings are understood as essentially individuals in a state of alienation or separation from each other, who are saved by entering into a social contract. How might 1:27 challenge this view?

6. Why would God decide to rest on the seventh day?

7. How can we practise equivalent 'rest' in our contemporary lives?

8. How does this view of creation challenge common contemporary assumptions about the world – eg luck or chance; astrology; the illusory nature of the physical world in some eastern religions; the rejection of the spiritual world in materialism?

Personal Application

God is a God of creativity, communication and action. The universe He has fashioned is a place of order and structure, but also complexity and variety, with space and freedom for His creatures to operate on His behalf. I can live in this world with a basic confidence in God's generosity and goodwill towards His creatures. In fact He has created me, together with other human beings, as the climax of His creation and given us a commission to bring the best out of, and look after, both the animate and inanimate creation. Fundamentally God looks favourably at all that He has made, me included, despite my weaknesses.

All this means that my behaviour towards other human beings is a form of behaving towards God; the extent to which I honour God is measured by the extent to which I honour other human beings, since they are made in God's image.

Seeing Jesus in the Scriptures

Like Genesis, John's Gospel begins with a prologue (John 1:1–18), and this presents Jesus as the Word of God, the agent by whom God created all that is. John's Gospel goes on to depict Jesus' creative power in turning water into wine (John 2:1–11) and multiplying loaves and fish (John 6:1–13).

As a man, Jesus is the ultimate image of God (2 Cor. 4:4; Col. 1:15). The creation is currently less than 'good', but if we want to know what God intends human beings to be, we can see Jesus, who was made a little lower than angels, now crowned with glory and honour (Heb. 2:9).

WEEK TWO

Humanity

Opening Icebreaker

Who has been to a special place – a garden or a wood, a
seashore or a mountain, a park or a zoo? What is the attraction
of such places? What are their dangers or temptations?

Bible Reading

- Genesis 2:4–25

Opening our Eyes

If the prologue provides a panoramic view of the creation of the entire cosmos, the first 'half' of Genesis opens with the story of the Garden of Eden. This is a careful literary work, moving through three scenes towards a central turning point, and then moving back through three corresponding scenes, each matching the earlier ones in reverse. This literary structure is very common in both Old and New Testaments, and reflects storytelling techniques in oral cultures.

Table 2.1 The Garden of Eden (Genesis 2:4–3:24)

2:4a   *toledoth* heading
2:4b–17   God forms man from ground, places him in garden; Eden described; God's permission andprohibition to man
2:18–25   God declares 'not good', forms animals, brings to man who names them; forms woman, brings to man – man's declaration
3:1–5   Serpent made by God; serpent & woman in dialogue
3:6–7   **Woman and man eat fruit**
3:8–13   Man & woman hide; God, man & woman in dialogue
3:14–21   God declares consequences for serpent, woman, man; Adam names Eve, God makes skin garments
3:22–24   God deliberates, drives man and woman out of the garden; cherubim placed to prevent their return to tree of life in Eden

In this study we focus on the early part of the story before discord sets in with the introduction of the serpent. The origin of human beings, summarised in the prologue, is explored further here. If human beings are created in God's image according to 1:27, the limitations of humanity's godlikeness are emphasised in 2:4–25.

In the prologue the creation of human beings was the climax

of God's acts, but in this account, God's formation of man seems to precede all else growing in the world (2:4–7). However, the NIV interprets the verb tense in 2:8 (cf v19) to indicate a previous divine act, so the man is placed in an already planted garden. It contains fruit-bearing trees – so God feeds man, not the other way round, as Babylonian stories of origin imagine.

The Garden of Eden (2:10–14) appears located north-east of Mesopotamia, although the rivers Gihon and Pishon are not easy to identify. However, the geography used here is not the modern topographical kind, but rather cosmological – this was God's sanctuary. Many features of this garden are symbolised later in Israel's tabernacle and Temple, eg in the ante-chamber to the holy of holies the seven-branched candlestick, or menorah, symbolised the tree of life (Exod. 25:31–40). The river of Eden informs later visions of the life-giving water flowing from the throne of God (Ezek. 47:1–12; Rev. 22:1–2).

The narrator returns to God's placing of the man in the garden (Gen. 2:15–17) – this time with a task to fulfil. For the first time in this passage God addresses the man – with permission to eat from any tree, but also with a prohibition concerning one fruit in particular.

The verdict of 'not good' on the man's solitary state (2:18) sounds a note of discord with the 'very good' verdict of the prologue (1:31) – it is clear that this man is a social being, something less than obvious in individualistic Western cultures. The naming of the animals demonstrates man's dominion over them (2:19–20) – they are potential companions, not dangers, nor to be exploited. But they are inadequate partners, so God finally creates woman from man, and introduces them in an archetypal wedding ceremony (2:21–25). The verdict is pronounced by the man, uttering the first poetry of the Bible. The narrator comments profoundly about marriage in general before observing this couple's comfortable relationship.

Discussion Starters

1. What clues to human nature are given in this passage?

2. The Garden of Eden remains a powerful concept in human psychology. What stands out about it in these verses?

3. How is God depicted in this passage?

4. How is the relationship between the man and animals envisaged in 2:18–20? What clues might this passage provide for contemporary treatment of animals – wildlife and endangered species, farming of domestic animals, the keeping of pets?

_____

_____

_____

_____

_____

_____

5. How is the marriage relationship envisaged in 2:18–25? What principles might this passage provide for contemporary intimate relationships?

_____

_____

_____

_____

_____

_____

Personal Application

We are encouraged here to see God as much more than a remote deity. He is actively involved with His creation (including me) – forming, breathing into, putting into, commanding, reflecting ('not good'), experimenting (with the animals), making a helper, bringing them together.

The threefold principle of 'leaving, uniting, one flesh' is vital. The marriage relationship takes precedence over old parental loyalties; it needs continual nurture, and must not be squeezed out by the clamour of children; it celebrates physical affection and sexual union (the latter to the exclusion of all others).

Seeing Jesus in the Scriptures

After the resurrection, Jesus 'breathed' on the disciples and said, 'Receive the Holy Spirit' (John 20:22), an echo of the original creation (Gen. 2:7). The gift of the Holy Spirit is something subsequent to the original gift of life; it is the sign of the start of the new creation.

Jesus' teaching about divorce goes back before Moses' permission to the creation principle of Genesis 2:24 (Mark 10:1–12; but see also the slightly different version in Matthew 19:1–12).

For Jews in Jesus' day, marriage was the norm, and so it is highly significant that Jesus did not get married (despite the ingenuity of Dan Brown's *The Da Vinci Code*!). However, He was certainly not an individualist since He formed close relationships with men and, remarkably, with women. Jesus' full humanity cut through the centuries of patriarchalism to embody the divine intention of respect, fascination and creativity sparked by the holy, delicate, wonder-generating interaction of women with men.

WEEK THREE

Dislocation

Opening Icebreaker

Many conventional Christian words, such as 'temptation', 'sinful' and 'wicked', have been subverted in secular speech so that they connote 'desirability', 'pleasure' and 'thrills'. What words remain to express what is wrong with the world and with humanity?

Bible Reading

- Genesis 3:1–24

Opening our Eyes

This study explores the outcome of the story of the Garden of Eden (see Table 2.1 for a reminder of the literary structure of the whole passage).

The serpent is very briefly introduced; although a wild animal, he appears more knowledgeable than the woman. He is characterised as 'crafty', but not sinister or magical. In fact this is an attribute considered worthy of pursuit in Proverbs 12:16; 13:16 (translated 'prudence'), though it can also be employed deviously (Exod. 21:14, translated 'scheme'). Ancient Israelites would have recognised the serpent as an evil influence without associating it with the ultimate source of evil. But by Jesus' day Jews had developed a stronger notion of Satan, and that adversary seems identified with the serpent in some New Testament texts (Rom. 16:20; Rev. 12:9).

The dominant Roman Catholic and Protestant traditions of understanding what went wrong here is disobedience. In eating the fruit, the woman and man went contrary to the divine prohibition in Genesis 2:17, and thus lost their original perfection. Sin has been understood according to the 'crime' model, emphasising wilful rebellion against God. Accordingly, salvation has been understood in terms of deliverance from guilt and punishment. While there is truth in this tradition, it does not fully reflect the biblical witness, nor does it provide a sufficient basis for Christian ministry in addressing human shortcomings and their consequences.

In the Eastern Orthodox tradition, God created the first pair in a state of immature innocence, with potential to be realised through a process of learning and growth. The first sin consisted of a failure to enter into the maturity God had intended. The serpent was not offering Eve anything new (compare Gen. 1:27); in fact, the first humans failed to exercise dominion over the serpent, which was merely one of the animals. Eve saw certain gains to be had by consuming the fruit, but did not consider the losses that would also result. Adam was silent and went along with Eve's decision. Thus people sin by omission as much as by commission; they fearfully fail to fulfil their potential, remain overly dependent upon others, and can be crippled by lack of confidence.

Underlying these two models of sin is a failure to trust God – either to believe His Word and comply with His limitations, or to take the initiative and begin to move towards maturity. The fundamental human problem is lack of faith in God, a fear that God has not done or will not do what is best for humanity. In general the outcome of sin is captured in the expressions 'missing the mark' or 'falling short of the glory of God' (Rom. 3:23).

The effect of sin is organically linked to what the man and woman had done – it produces its own consequences. The intimacy between them is shattered and they hide from God. He seeks them out but they try to displace their blame. God pronounces the consequences of their action, and they are expelled from the garden. Thus death (exclusion from God's dwelling place – leading eventually to physical death) is traced back to the first human couple, whereas Babylonian stories assigned the origin of universal death to the time of the Flood.

Discussion Starters

1. What strategies does the serpent employ in Genesis 3:1–5? How effective is Eve's response in verses 2–3? In what senses is the serpent truthful, and in what senses is he devious?

2. What does or doesn't go on in the mind of the woman in verse 6? – and of the man (NB v17)? What is the immediate effect of their eating on their relationship (v7)?

3. How do relationships break down in verses 8–13?

4. In what tone of voice do you imagine God speaking in verses 14–19? Where might He be angry and where sorrowful? What factors of an imperfect world do these speeches explain?

5. What elements of grace and hope can be found in
this passage?

_____

_____

_____

_____

_____

6. Why does God take such drastic action in verses 22–24?

_____

_____

_____

_____

_____

7. What overall insights does this story give us into human
nature and sinfulness?

_____

_____

_____

_____

_____

Personal Application

Human life offers many opportunities to grow and mature. Crises occur when we must either move forward or shrivel. Sometimes we think we know better than God, and go contrary to His Word. On other occasions we may fail to take the initiative that would be an appropriate exercise of God's likeness.

Sometimes I suffer as a result of other people's sins, and they suffer as a result of mine. Sin works out its consequences in my relationship with God, other people and the world around – not just at an individual level, but at a corporate level. Sin often has unintended and unforeseen consequences – we are not so clever and good at solving our problems as we like to think.

Seeing Jesus in the Scriptures

Jesus faced temptation at the start of His ministry (Mark 1:12–13). Further temptations or tests are apparent in Mark 8:11–12; 8:31–33 and 14:32–42. In Matthew's account of the first of these (4:1–11), Jesus takes control of the devil by appeal to God's Word addressed to the Israelites in the wilderness before they entered the promised land (Deut. 8:3; 6:13,16). The devil could also quote Scripture (Psa. 91:11–12) as a half-truth, but Jesus succeeds because He employs a passage that resonates with His own situation (40 days in the wilderness echoes the Israelites' 40 years).

The book of Hebrews encourages us to hold firmly to the faith we profess because Jesus understands our weaknesses and has come through temptation on our behalf (Heb. 4:14–16).

WEEK FOUR

Violence

Opening Icebreaker

Bring some recent newspapers to the group and look in them for examples of both incredulity and horror at human violence.

Bible Reading

- Genesis 4:1–26

Opening our Eyes

The birth of children to Adam and Eve leads quickly into the story of the first murder and its aftermath (Gen. 4:1–16). An account of Cain's descendants follows (4:17–24), before the birth of a third son to Adam and Eve is recorded (4:25–26). Thus Genesis 4 ends with an echo of its beginning, and its literary structure is shown in Table 4.1.

Table 4.1 The Development of Violence (Genesis 4:1–26)

4:1–2 Children for Adam and Eve; the Lord's help
4:3–5 The sacrifices of Cain and Abel
4:6–7 The Lord speaks with Cain
4:8 **Cain murders Abel**
4:9–14 The Lord in dialogue with Cain
4:15–16 The Lord's sanctions against killing Cain; he departs
4:17–22 Cain's descendants, cultural developments
4:23–24 Lamech's disproportionate vengeance
4:25–26 Another child for Adam and Eve; calling on the Lord

Despite the tragedy of expulsion from Eden, the help of the Lord in bringing Eve's first child to birth is acknowledged. God continues to play a major part in the life of the first family. The second child's birth is briefly told to set the scene for the major action. The name Abel translates from Hebrew as 'a puff of wind', meaning 'insubstantial' or 'transient' (it forms the refrain 'meaninglessness' in Ecclesiastes).

When Cain and Abel have grown up they both bring offerings (or tribute) to the Lord; Cain from his crops and Abel from his flock. Why does God favour Abel's offering rather than Cain's? The only significant difference between the brothers' offerings lies, not in their kind (animal vs vegetable), but in their quality – Abel brought *fat portions* from some of the *firstborn*. But not all commentators are convinced that God's approval was geared to the quality of offerings.

Divine disapproval stirs Cain to intense anger due to 'loss of face', but not yet to sin, as is evident in the Lord's speech to Cain. He names Cain's disposition and indicates that Cain may still be accepted if he does 'what is right' – God's disapproval was not final. But an ugly alternative lurks close at hand – Cain must master his resentment lest it conquer him. What a fascinating characterisation of sin! What an appalling freedom of choice! However, Cain succumbs to temptation, takes his brother away from the home, and murders him.

When challenged by the Lord, Cain seeks to shrug off responsibility, but God insists that such a heinous crime carries heavy consequences. No law against murder has yet been promulgated, yet it is assumed that Cain should know such an action is wrong. The curse reinforces that pronounced to Adam (3:17–19), leaving Cain a restless wanderer. Cain anticipates being a marked man (a significant population is presumed at this point). In response, God shows His displeasure at the idea that a murderer is a legitimate target of violence, and marks Cain specifically to warn off avengers. Cain departs from the presence of the Lord.

Cain marries (again a significant population is presumed), and his descendants are given in a genealogy that includes some references to cultural origins (4:17–22). Lamech is singled out for his vicious speech (4:23–24) that twists God's pronouncement at 4:15 into a justification for extreme retaliation. The chapter ends with a reversion to the birth of Adam and Eve's third son (named by his father this time), and in turn his son (4:25–26), together with a mention of prayer.

Discussion Starters

1. What insights into human resentment and guilt emerge from the story of Cain and Abel? How are sin and its conquest portrayed? Does this help us in dealing with powerful temptations today?

_____

_____

_____

_____

_____

2. According to this account, why is the taking of human life prohibited? What are the consequences when it happens?

_____

_____

_____

_____

_____

3. In what way does Lamech's speech twist God's warning in 4:15? What is the long-term impact of Cain's sin on his descendants?

_____

_____

_____

_____

_____

4. 'History begins with murder... every murder is fratricide, because all men are brothers' (Herbert Chanan Brichto). How significant is this chapter in understanding and exposing human evil?

_____

_____

_____

_____

_____

5. We may think that we could never commit murder or exact vengeance. However, Jesus urges us to reflect upon the links between anger and murder (Matt. 5:21–22). How may we harbour resentments that are as corrosive as physical violence?

_____

_____

_____

_____

_____

Personal Application

A later writer said that Abel offered God a better sacrifice than Cain 'by faith', and was commended as a righteous man (Heb. 11:4). His life was cut short, appeared meaningless, but because of his faith 'he still speaks'. Anthony Walker was a young Christian, brutally murdered by a racist in Liverpool in 2005. At the conclusion of his murderer's trial, his mother publicly forgave the man. The faith of Anthony and his mother speaks to us today.

In contrast with Cain, Christians should learn to recognise the sin that crouches at the door, and to seek the transforming work of the Holy Spirit so that we may love our brothers and sisters in particular, tangible ways (1 John 3:12).

Seeing Jesus in the Scriptures

In a fascinating chapter dealing with the conduct of relationships in the Church, Jesus emphasises the need for repeated forgiveness (Matt. 18:21–22). Seven times is not enough – seventy-seven times is more like it. This is not any old large number, but an echo and repudiation of Lamech's boast (Gen. 4:24). Jesus' teaching and modelling of forgiveness go to the root of human strife. Revenge is typical of so much human behaviour – in soap operas, in sport, in the workplace. Jesus calls the Church to a different path that reflects His own way of dealing with hate, malice and the abuse of power.

WEEK FIVE

Judgment and salvation

Opening Icebreaker

Has anyone seen a disaster movie? What themes and characters are common in such films? Why can such films be so popular?

Bible Readings

- Genesis 6:1–8
- Genesis 6:9–7:24

Opening our Eyes

In this session we concentrate on the first half of the Flood account that begins with the heading at Genesis 6:9 up to the death of all living animals, leaving the resolution of it to next week. But we will start with the short passage 6:1-8 that serves as a prelude to this judgment on sin, though standing outside its formal structure.

In several Old Testament passages God is pictured in heaven as 'holding court' among minor 'deities' (eg 1 Kings 22:19-22; Psa. 82). Here the sexual behaviour of certain of these minor 'deities' is not explicitly condemned, yet it provokes God to reduce the human lifespan. It also seems to contribute to the divine verdict on humanity's accumulated wickedness in Genesis 6:5 – notice that the full implications of Genesis 3 have only now come to fruition. The narrator provides an extraordinary window on the impact that this has on God: feelings of grief and pain – note the contrast between the human heart and the divine heart in 6:5-6. There is also a soliloquy in which God contemplates wiping out all life. Yet one man was different, and his righteousness even carries over into the start of the new literary section (6:9), and tempers the whole judgment story. The Fall did not make blamelessness impossible, and for Noah's sake God tempers judgment with salvation (cf Gen. 18:20-25).

There are disagreements about how best to understand the literary structure of 6:9-9:19, but there is sufficient symmetry about it to suggest Table 5.1. This literary structure emphasises the death of all life as the culmination of God's judgment. Next week we will pick up from the turning point where God remembers Noah.The reasons for God's judgment are doubly stated by the narrator in 6:11-12. God emphatically informs Noah of His decision to send the Flood on account of human violence in 6:13. Brief instructions for building the ark are given in order that representatives will escape the coming inundation (6:14–16). The judgment is declared once more, but God explains to Noah what he must do next in view of the covenant that already exists, but remains to be confirmed (6:18). This is the first appearance of this key biblical term and will be discussed further in Genesis 9.

Table 5.1 The Flood story

6:9a   *toledoth* heading
6:9b–10   Noah and his three sons
6:11–12   God sees all the earth is corrupt
6:13–22   God's instructions to Noah
7:1–9   God commands Noah to enter the ark
7:10–16   Flood begins, ark is closed
7:17–20   Waters increase
7:21–24   **All life on earth dies**
8:1–5   Waters recede
8:6–14   Flood ends, ark's window opens
8:15–22   God commands Noah to exit the ark
9:1–7   God's instructions to Noah
9:8–17   God promises never again to destroy
9:18–19   Noah's three sons

The stipulation that a male and female of every kind should be taken into the ark is adjusted in God's second speech, becoming seven pairs of every kind of clean animal plus one pair of unclean animals and seven pairs of every bird (7:2–3). There is a reversion to pairs of clean and unclean of birds and animals in the note of Noah's age and the account of his entry into the ark, along with his family and the animals (7:6–9). These details are virtually repeated with a few extra details in 7:11–16. Notice how Noah does exactly as he is commanded (6:22; 7:5,9,16).Finally the effects of the rising flood are enumerated: water covers the mountains, yet the ark floats, carrying its precious cargo. Every other living thing is wiped out.

 **Discussion Starters**

1. Why would God object to the behaviour in Genesis 6:1–4? Does Genesis 1 provide any clues? Might there be any equivalent objectionable behaviour in our world?

2. This passage contains the first reference to a divine emotion in the Bible (6:6–7). What do you make of God's reaction to the way His world has turned out?

3. Why is God so offended at corruption and violence (6:11–13) that He decides to destroy the earth? Why are Noah and his family given a means of survival?

4. How is the fate of the animals tied to the fate of human beings in the Flood account? Does this observation have any contemporary implications?

5. How does the description of the Flood process link to the original creation story? What does this imply?

_____

_____

_____

_____

_____

6. God's judgment is not a popular subject, even among Christians. How does the Flood help us to understand it?

_____

_____

_____

_____

7. In the contemporary world what reactions do you notice to major disasters? How might Christians respond to such disasters, and to such reactions to them?

_____

_____

_____

_____

_____

Personal Application

Sometimes people feel revulsion at the human evil they observe in the world, and wonder why God does not act to deal with it. This account tells us that God feels that revulsion too – indeed His 'first impulse' is to wipe out the human race along with all life. God is fully aware of what such a drastic course of action entails – death, death everywhere. Yet this thoroughly just God recognises Noah's righteousness and saves him, along with representatives of the animal kingdom.

In this whole account Noah does not utter a word; it is his obedience that speaks volumes. He built the ark 'by faith... in holy fear' (Heb. 11:7) – so his obedience sprang out of his faith – his outlook on life was formed out of a healthy attention to God.

Noah is saved, not *from* the Flood, but through the Flood. God does not isolate me from the perils of living in a world subject to judgment, but grants me a means of living through those perils.

Seeing Jesus in the Scriptures

Jesus did not come to judge the world (John 12:47), but to save it through His own life, death and resurrection. However, a day is coming when He will return as judge of the earth (2 Tim. 4:1). Jesus warns His disciples about the unexpectedness of His future coming; it will be 'as in the days of Noah'. So we are called to keep watch and be ready for His coming (Matt. 24:37–44).

WEEK SIX

Covenant

Opening Icebreaker

Think of the most solemn promises or commitments you have made or seen others make. What is involved in keeping such commitments?

Bible Reading

- Genesis 8:1–9:19

Opening our Eyes

We pick up the story of the Flood at its turning point. For a reminder of the literary structure of the whole passage, see Table 5.1.

'But God remembered Noah' (8:1) – the verb for memory has connotations of care, concern and cherishing, rather than recovery from a mental lapse. God's wind, which had hovered over the waters in Genesis 1:2 (there translated 'Spirit'), and which elsewhere turns sea into dry land (Exod. 14:21–22), here causes the waters to recede.

Noah's sending out of the birds (Gen. 8:6–12) has very strong parallels with the Mesopotamian flood story in the *Gilgamesh Epic*. At one point, its hero meets a character called Utnapishtim who has joined the assembly of the gods. In response to Gilgamesh's enquiry, Utnapishtim tells the following rather ironic story.

The god Enlil is tired of the noisiness of humanity, and because of their inconvenience he decides to wipe them out by means of a flood. However, another god, Ea, communicates with one of his devotees, instructing him to build a ship that will enable its occupants to escape the flood. The dimensions of this boat are those of a huge cube, and it is completed in seven days. Utnapishtim loads the craft with provisions, his family and animals. When the horrifying rains begin, even the gods are frightened by the deluge. The storm lasts for seven days before the flood abates; the boat settles on Mount Nimush. After seven days, Utnapishtim lets out a series of birds to see if the dry land is habitable; a dove, followed by a swallow, go out and return, but a raven does not return. Utnapishtim lets everyone out of the ship and offers a sacrifice to the gods – who delightedly swarm around it, having become hungry through lack of human attention.

Enlil arrives and is angry that people have survived the flood, but Ea manages to pacify him. Utnapishtim is granted a sort of immortality.

Perhaps the most striking difference between the Bible's Flood account and the *Gilgamesh Epic* is the sovereignty of God, emphasised by Noah's dependence upon God. Although Noah's initiative with the birds demonstrates that the Flood has receded, and he removes the ark's covering, he does not leave the vessel until God instructs him to do so (8:15–19).

Still without a recorded utterance, Noah offers a sacrifice. This prompts a divine soliloquy made up of a double self-limitation of judgment, even as the Lord recognises the incorrigibility of the human heart (8:20–22). At the close of this judgment story humankind has not changed, but God has.

Next God addresses an extensive series of speeches to Noah, beginning with an echo of 1:28 (9:1,7). However, a significant shift is introduced in the relationship between humans and animals, including permission for human consumption of animals. The seriousness of the taking of human life (even by animals) is also emphasised, reflecting the earlier concern about violence (6:9).

Second (9:8–11), God's earlier deliberation is declared to Noah and his sons in the form of a binding commitment, to human beings and animals. This establishment or confirmation of covenant (first mentioned at 6:18) is momentous, and finds echoes later in Genesis (15:18; 17:2) and elsewhere in the Old Testament.

Third (9:12–17), God provides a sign of His covenant in the form of a rainbow – He hangs up His war-bow. Remarkably this is not a reminder to human beings, so much as to God.

Discussion Starters

1. Noah's sending out of the birds is one of only two initiatives that he takes (without divine instruction) in the whole story. The other is to build an altar and offer sacrifice. What purpose do these actions serve in the story, and what might we learn from them?

2. God's soliloquy in Genesis 8:21 answers that in 6:6–7. In what way has God changed in this story?

3. What does God's statement in 9:6 contribute to the debate about the death penalty? How should we interpret this verse in relation to God's declaration concerning Cain (4:15)?

4. What does the word 'covenant' convey to us? What binding agreements do people make today? Do they help us understand God's covenants (here and elsewhere in the Bible)?

_____

_____

_____

_____

_____

5. Some global watchers think that the current world population is too great for its resources to sustain. Does this mean that the command to 'be fruitful and multiply, and fill the earth' has been accomplished and thus careful thought must be given to restricting population growth in the future?

_____

_____

_____

_____

_____

Personal Application

Noah's obedience to God provides an example of responsiveness to His word. Noah is not completely passive; he keeps alert to what is happening to the world beyond the ark, and acknowledges God has been their deliverer. Paul challenges us 'in view of God's mercy, to offer' our 'bodies as living sacrifices, holy and pleasing to God', which is our spiritual 'worship' (Rom. 12:1–2).

God's commitment to the world, symbolised by His rainbow, does not mean that we sit back and do nothing about the threats to the world that exist today (some of human origin, eg global warming). If God is thoroughly committed to His world, then so should His children be. God calls me to be actively concerned about poverty, over-consumption, pollution, conservation and recycling.

Seeing Jesus in the Scriptures

Jesus' death brought to an end the continual cycle of blood for blood – if only we could see it. The cross of Jesus stood, not in the clouds, but firmly in the earth, bringing the peace of God into the blood-spattered reality of human evil.

Jesus spoke of the new covenant in His blood (eg Luke 22:20). When Christians take part in the Lord's Supper (or Holy Communion) we remember what God has done to deal with the alienation between ourselves and God. Less often do we remember that the body of Christ Jesus brings hostility between human beings to an end (Eph. 2:14–18).

Jesus calls His followers to go beyond rejection of murder to commitment to reconciliation (Matt 5:21–26), and even to love of enemies (Matt 5:43–48).

WEEK SEVEN

Disrespect and confusion

Opening Icebreaker

Bring some newspapers to the group, and together look for stories of disrespect, human pride and confusion. It is always easier to spot such failings in others while failing to acknowledge them in ourselves.

Bible Readings

- Genesis 9:20–29
- Genesis 11:1–9
- Genesis 11:27–12:3

Opening our Eyes

We might think that God's renewal of creation after the Flood would mean that Noah and his wife would walk off into a rosy future. But we have already seen God's realism about human evil (Gen. 8:21). The last story of Noah and his sons confirms this point at the individual level, and leads into extensive genealogies that sketch the repopulation of the earth after the Flood (see 10:32). The narrative concerning the Tower of Babel confirms the point about human evil at a social level. Thus the first half of Genesis draws to a close, leaving readers with a question: 'What can God do to recover His creation that repeatedly lapses from His intentions?' The second 'half' of Genesis provides the beginnings of God's answer; we will conclude with a sneak preview of it in the first verses of Abraham's story.

Whereas Noah's ancestors had grown only basic foods, Noah now introduces the cultivation of a vineyard. It may be that the remark of Noah's father at 5:29 applies here – wine may comfort those engaged in hard labour. However, wine can also lead to drunkenness.

The chief moral concern in this passage is not drunkenness, but the behaviour of Ham. Respect for a person in ancient Israel involved the covering of sexual parts of the body, so that seeing someone naked constituted an extreme dishonouring of them (remember Gen. 3:21; cf 2 Sam. 6:16,20). In the ancient world, honouring parents was a sacred duty, and an Israelite would have agreed with a Ugaritic epic that stipulates that a son should take his father 'by the hand when he's drunk, carry him when he is sated with wine'. The honouring attitude of the other two sons is emphasised in verse 23.

For the first time in the Bible Noah speaks – and it is to utter a curse! Earlier God had cursed the snake and the ground (3:14,17), but not the woman or the man explicitly. Perhaps Noah's anger at Ham was understandable, but his curses went too far. Jacob would later utter more measured curses and blessings on his sons (49:1–28).

The story of the Tower of Babel follows the recounting of the establishment of multiple cultural and linguistic groups (10:4,20,31). This observation supports the view that the common speech in 11:1 reflects, not an idyllic primal language, but the Neo-Assyrian practice of imposing the conqueror's tongue on subjected peoples. The construction project (like many today) is about building reputation, and represents an expression of power over others – slaves would have done the hard work!

There is great irony in the Lord's needing to 'come down' in order to see this skyscraper. Such human self-aggrandisement does not threaten God, but the human race *is* threatened by the imposition of artificial unity.

Thus God's confusing of the builders' language should not be understood as a simple punishment – rather it is a fundamentally restorative move. His scattering of peoples furthers His creation intention that humanity should 'fill the earth' (1:28; 9:1).

The second 'half' of Genesis begins with the account of Terah (11:27). This starts with a major journey marked by death and barrenness. In this context, Abram hears God's command, several promises and final goal. From hereon God's strategy to recover the whole creation consists of calling one particular family or people to whom He will reveal Himself intimately so that they begin to reflect His character and bring His blessing to the rest of humanity.

Discussion Starters

1. While the details of the last Noah story may be puzzling, what might the author have wanted to convey to readers by including it?

2. In the nineteenth century, defenders of slavery drew from Genesis 9:26–27 a justification for the enslavement of some African peoples, descended from Ham. What do you think of this kind of biblical interpretation?

3. If the Tower of Babel story is an exposure of human arrogance at a social level, what might be the equivalent of such tower building today?

4. It appears that Abram [Abraham] was already on a journey to Canaan when God called him to leave his country (11:31; 12:1). What difficulties had his family already encountered by then?

5. In what ways does God's famous speech to Abraham (12:1–3) connect with the early chapters of Genesis that we have studied?

_____

_____

_____

_____

6. Paul taught early Gentile disciples of Jesus that Abraham was their father in faith (eg Rom. 4). How might contemporary Christians understand the implications of this speech for them?

_____

_____

_____

_____

7. Are there any observations we would want to make on Genesis 1–11 as a whole?

_____

_____

_____

_____

Personal Application

The righteous Noah copes with an extraordinary period of intense activity followed by enforced rest (apart from feeding the animals!). It is when he gets to relax that things go wrong – too much wine, a cheeky younger generation (but they weren't all like that) and, awaking with a hangover, he utters a curse. Father and son are at loggerheads. How do I cope with the ups and downs of life, the stresses and strains of family relationships?

In what ways do contemporary societies and leaders seek to make names for themselves (or 'leave a legacy')? – and who is exploited in the process? Do I seek to impose an artificial unity in my neighbourhood, workplace, or church group? How can I reflect the manifold wisdom of God in appreciating the rich diversity of His creation (Eph. 3:10)?

Seeing Jesus in the Scriptures

In Matthew's Gospel, Jesus encounters a descendant of Canaan, a representative of Israel's old seductive enemies (Matt. 15:21–28). Yet her extraordinary faith contributes to His revision of Jewish attitudes to old adversaries (also including Samaritans and Romans). Jesus radically revises the curses of the Old Testament.

The gift of the Holy Spirit on the Day of Pentecost (Acts 2) made possible what ancient empires had sought to impose – the communication of the gospel of Jesus Christ, bringing about a genuine human unity while celebrating the variety of God's gifts to humanity.

God's speech to Abraham ('Go to a land...') finds an echo and a transformation in Jesus' parting words to His disciples in Matthew 28:19 ('Go and make disciples of all nations...').

Leader's Notes

Week One: Creation

The aims of this session are:

- To begin to generate a sense of a group studying the Bible together.
- To provide a feel for how the book of Genesis works as a whole, and chapters 1–11 in particular.
- To discuss how the prologue portrays God and the creation, together with contemporary implications.

Begin with introductions (if people do not know each other) and use the Icebreaker. The point of this is that, although Genesis 1–11 may seem familiar, readers need to be aware that it reflects an ancient and foreign culture. In particular, it is not a modern scientific account of cosmic beginnings.

Next read the Introduction to the group to enable people to get some perspective on this first part of the book of Genesis. A number of issues are raised that may generate discussion: science and evolution, authorship and ancient culture. You may need to allow time for expression of different opinions, but not too much! The Introduction also suggests that these chapters engage with questions of 'empire' – and thus invites discussion of contemporary equivalents.

Genesis 1–11 provides a universal frame of reference for God's people – ancient Israel and the Church. It is likely that Israel understood Genesis 1–11 to refer to what happened in the past, but also to reflect human life in every age. For example, Genesis 3 tells a story about the past, subsequent to the creation, when sin emerged into the life of the world, but it also functions as a typical encounter with the reality of temptation.

Coming to the passage for the first week, ask two or three people to read Genesis 1:1–2:3 aloud. Some guidance can be given to the group by reading the section Opening Our Eyes. It may help to explore the literary structure of the prologue as set out in Table I.1, and to discuss the way in which it addressed Mesopotamian stories of origins.

Use the Discussion Starters to explore what the passage says about God and God's creation of the world, and to explore contemporary implications. The Personal Application section shows how the prologue can have quite specific implications for life today. Some of the most obvious connections with the New Testament are made in the section Seeing Jesus in the Scriptures.

Further details

Genesis 1:1 is translated as an independent sentence in the NIV It is best understood as a summary of the whole passage. Verse 2 describes the conditions before the first creative act in verse 3; God's creative work begins with already existing 'raw material', an earth that was 'formless and empty'. Sometimes this has been interpreted to mean that God had already defeated forces of evil chaos before the first day. However, the expression simply means something like 'an undifferentiated mass'.

The meaning of the expression 'in our image, in our likeness' (1:26) has been the subject of much debate. Some have thought that certain human capacities (speech, intelligence, etc) reflect divine capacities, and it has been suggested that the male–female relationship reflects some divine qualities. It is most likely that this expression refers to human rule on God's behalf in creation (as in v28). Human beings are like God in exercising royal power on earth, but also God delegated to humans a share in His rule of the earth. NB the father–son relationship is one in which a son comes to be a repetition of his father (cf Adam and Seth in Gen. 5:3).

One implication is that the human race enjoys an essential unity, challenging the common view that humans are alienated from each other.

In conclusion, pray together.

Week Two: Humanity

Aims:
- To develop the sense of the group getting to know each other and studying the Bible together. The Icebreaker should help this and lead into the garden story.
- To discuss how the second creation story portrays humanity and God, together with contemporary implications.

The creation of human beings, mentioned first in 1:26–30, is given a more extensive treatment in 2:4–25. The material in this session may be less time-consuming than in the first week, so if significant matters were unfinished then, they could be given some time here.

In verse 7, the close relationship between the man and his world is emphasised by the similarity of two Hebrew words: 'the man' (adam) is created from 'the ground' (adamah). 'Ground' and 'dust' (v7) serve to emphasise the fragility of humanity and the total dependence of the creature on the Creator. In this story, humanity possesses no inherent immortality, no spark of the divine that removes him from his earthy existence. The man is simply given breath by God, something that he shares with animals.

God provides trees in the garden for aesthetic pleasure as well as for food (2:9). Eden contains precious materials (2:11–12). Just one prohibition is given with a warning (2:16–17).

In this passage there are some indications of the processes God employs in creation: 'forming, breathing into, planting'. Remarkably, the finding of a suitable companion involves some experimentation on God's part; the animals do not quite fit the bill, so the more extraordinary task of creating woman from man is undertaken. Twice God lets the human being decide whether the animals or the woman is 'suitable for him'. Extraordinarily, God is portrayed as placing Himself at the service of the 'good' of the human being.

The Discussion Starters raise questions about human treatment of animals and about intimate relationships. However, it is important to remember that Genesis 1–2 is not a complete account of creation for contemporary readers. A fully biblical approach to such subjects would require consideration of many other passages and interpretive moves.

The act of naming was understood in the ancient world as indicating authority over the one named, just as the disclosure of one's name gave a certain power into the possession of the recipient (eg see the dynamics at play in Genesis 32:24–29). Thus the naming of the animals indicates human dominion over the animal kingdom (cf 1:28). Some have argued that such biblical passages are to be blamed for human mistreatment of animals and the current environmental crisis. However, the proper emphasis here would be on stewardship and responsibility.

Historically, Genesis 2 has frequently been employed to subordinate women to men. The argument ran that the man was formed first, and the woman, coming second, was of less importance, merely his 'helper' (2:18). We can observe Paul subverting this kind of argument in 1 Corinthians 11:7–12 (though he does not in 1 Timothy 2:13–14). To the chauvinistic interpretation, the reply may be made that in the Genesis prologue human beings are created as the final and climactic act of God, so that the equivalent order of priority in Genesis 2 would make woman more important than man! (Anyway, in 1:27 male and female are given equal status as God's image and likeness.) Furthermore, God Himself is described elsewhere as Israel's 'help' (Psa. 33:20; 70:5; 115:9–11), thus such a term in no way belittles woman compared to man.

In conclusion, discuss how a passage like this can shape our prayers, and pray as a group.

Week Three: Dislocation

Aims:
- To develop further the sense of the group studying the Bible together – more than a bunch of individuals. The Icebreaker should help people to think about contemporary use of language and lead into the subject.
- To explore how the story of the first sin helps to understand several facets of sinfulness today.

People may think that they know this story well, but it is important to read it carefully and to explore its meaning with the help of various Christian traditions. Some pointers have been included in Opening Our Eyes.

Elements of grace and hope have been identified in two places. God's making of garments for Adam and Eve (Gen. 3:21), indicates His continued concern for them, but it also entails the death of animals, pointing to the future sacrificial system in which the life of animals makes humans fit for God's presence. Christians see here a prefiguring of Jesus' life laid down to reclothe us. God's pronouncement to the serpent, 'he will crush your head' (v15), is interpreted as a reference to the triumph of Jesus Christ over Satan.

Make sure that the group includes some discussion of the way this passage illuminates contemporary temptations and the outworkings of human sin (Discussion Starter 7). If people are comfortable enough with each other, they may be prepared to talk frankly about struggles with temptations – either to grasp at illicit pleasures, or to fail in the bold assertion of appropriate authority. But if the group members do not yet trust each other enough, there could be more general reflection on human weakness, perhaps as portrayed in the media. The outworking of sin's consequences could also be considered in parallel with God's pronouncements in 3:14–19.

One subject that may arise in discussion, especially as connections may be made to the New Testament, is the doctrine of original sin. This is the idea that Adam's sin was transmitted automatically to his descendants. One of the most influential theologians, Augustine of Hippo (a north African who lived between AD 354 and AD 430), thought that the fallen nature of Adam was transmitted biologically through sexual procreation, and thus that even babies were sinners. This idea was based upon a poor Latin translation of Romans 5:12: 'Therefore, *just as* sin entered the world through one man, and death through sin, *so also* death came to all men, *in whom* all sinned.' A better translation of the final Greek phrase highlighted here would be '*because* all sinned', emphasising the *analogy* between the consequences of Adam's sin and the sin of each of his descendants, rather than an automatic transmission of guilt. Paul is developing the analogy between Adam and Christ in Romans 5:12–21. But Christ's saving act does not automatically bring salvation to every human being; instead it establishes salvation as a potential for all – to be appropriated by faith. Likewise, Adam's sinful act does not automatically make every person a sinner. It is simply that, prior to his or her identification with Christ, a person is identified with Adam – as a sinner.

The great medieval theologian, Thomas Aquinas, maintained that the fall of humankind could not have entailed the loss of human reason. However, the Reformers were more pessimistic, believing that human reason was fallen along with every other aspect of humanity. Calvin related original sin not so much to heredity as to a judgment of God passed on all humankind. This was not to imply that human beings were incapable of doing good things, but it entailed the conviction that no aspect of humanity was unaffected by sin.

Discuss how this study can be turned into group prayer, and conclude in that way.

Week Four: Violence

Aims:

- By now people should be getting to know each other, but are there some who could contribute more? Or are there others who need to allow more space for quieter members to contribute? What more could be done to help them develop as a group?
- To explore how the story of the first violence helps to understand violence today, and the Christian call to renounce it.

This chapter introduces a major theme of Genesis: fraternal conflict. The later struggles between Ishmael and Isaac, Esau and Jacob, come to a climax between Joseph and his brothers, and they are reflected in serious tensions between the chosen family and outsiders (Gen. 26; 34).

At a number of points this story appears to presume a significant population of human beings: Cain's fear that he will be killed, his marriage, his building of a city. This is not easy to explain if he was literally one of three human beings at the time. It may be that some time/generation compression has occurred in the storytelling.

Cain's fear of being killed reflects the conventions of (later) Israelite society. A crime against an individual was a crime against his kinship group. Punishment was exacted by the victim's group, normally by a member of that family or clan called 'the redeemer of blood'. If the offender's group refused to deliver him for punishment, all members of that group became 'fair game', and the result might be a vendetta or war. Thus justice consisted of vengeance, and the certainty that vengeance would be pursued was the primary deterrent to murder. A member of the group who committed a serious offence against the group's standards was normally punished by being declared an outlaw or outcast rather than being executed, but he was then 'as good as dead'.

Cain's response to God's pronouncement of sentence is to point out that banishment might as well be a death sentence. God responds that he will visibly mark Cain so that he becomes Cain's 'redeemer of blood'. It is clear that God does not approve of vengeance. Some have argued from this against the death penalty for murder, though the opposite conclusion is often drawn from Genesis 9:6 (see Week Six). However, a Christian discussion of this subject would have to take Jesus' teaching fully into account.

The leader needs to get the group beyond expressions of horror at senseless murder or genocide and warfare (important as these are) to consider the potential in each of us to behave in ways that deny responsibility for our fellow human beings. Thus Discussion Starter 5 should help to see how Jesus perceived this worked in practice.

This guide does not include a study of Genesis 5 for reasons of space, but the leader may find that someone spots interesting parallels between its genealogies and those of Genesis 4 (Table 4.2).

Table 4.2 Parallel genealogies

Genesis 5:1–32	Genesis 4:25–26
Adam	Adam
Seth	Seth
Enosh	Enosh
	Genesis 4:17–22
Kenan**	Cain**
Mahalalel	Enoch*
Jared**	Irad**
Enoch*	Mehujael
Methuselah**	Methushael**
Lamech*	Lamech*
Noah	Jabal, Jubal/Tubal-Cain, Naamah

Key: * Identical names
  ** Similar names in Hebrew

Scholars have recognised that some traditional societies preserve variants of important genealogies. It is likely that the differences between these genealogies in Genesis must have been significant enough for the compiler to include them both. However, it is not clear what conclusions can be drawn from these observations

Help the group to find ways of turning discussion of violence into prayer and action that makes for peace.

Week Five: Judgment and Salvation

Aims:
- To continue to develop the group so that they listen to each other's contributions and discover how God can speak

through and to a group of His people.
- To explore how this story of God's judgment helps to understand His verdict on human evil, but also His determination to save humanity as well as the wider world.

The 'sons of God' incident is somewhat cryptic and may puzzle some people. The main reason for God's displeasure would be the transgression of boundaries between human beings and these divine beings (NB Genesis 1 sets up significant boundaries). In contrast with these characters, we will see that Noah recognises the difference between clean and unclean animals.

There has been a long history of biblical interpretation that refuses to take seriously the attribution of feelings to God. Some early theologians denied that God experienced emotions, such as grief or anger, since they thought this would involve His being vulnerable to His creation, and thus less than perfect. Furthermore, since the eighteenth-century enlightenment, Western cultures have tended (until very recently) to privilege reason over against emotion. But what if God chose to make Himself vulnerable to His creatures as part of entering into genuine relationships with them? It is true that God's emotions are not exactly like those of humans, just as His thoughts are not like our thoughts (Isa. 55:8), but this difference is one of appropriateness, rather than one of kind. God experiences and expresses emotions even more passionately than human beings, but He does so fully self-aware, and without taint of insecurity or enmity (eg Hos. 11:1–9).

What of the cause and extent of the actual Flood behind the stories? Various possibilities have been suggested:

- There was a worldwide catastrophe in which the great majority of human beings were killed. It is difficult to comprehend how enough water could have arrived on the scene to cause a flood that would cover major mountains, or where it would have gone afterwards. The concepts of 'the springs of the great deep, and the floodgates of the heavens' (Gen. 7:11) are foreign to scientific explanation.

- However, flood stories of this catastrophic kind exist around the world. Could a major meteorite strike or earthquake have caused a huge tsunami? How would an ark survive in such an event?
- At the end of the last ice-age, the sea level would have risen and flooded previously habitable areas below what we know as the shores of the Black Sea and Persian Gulf. These might have given rise to memories of a steadily rising flood, but there would have been no re-emergence of inundated areas afterwards.
- Mesopotamia suffered occasional river flooding due to high rainfall. Although such floods might be locally devastating, why might memories of them be turned into stories of a universal flood?

It is likely that the author took two earlier Israelite versions of a story about a disastrous flood that was well known in the ancient world, and combined them (allowing some repetitions to remain, as we have seen). The effect was to explain the Flood in terms of God's judgment on human corruption and violence, but also to emphasise God's grace in delivering representatives of the human race and animal kingdom from the disaster.

No contemporary disaster can really be compared with the Flood, since God has promised never to repeat it. So how might the group turn this study into prayer?

Week Six: Covenant

Aims:

- Hopefully the group is now working together well, even though it may contain strong differences of opinion. Get them to consider that this series of studies will soon draw to a close. What would they like to do next?
- To explore how the conclusion of the Flood story further fills out God's character, and the implications that this entails for human conduct.

We cannot be sure of the reason for the similarities between the Mesopotamian flood stories and the one in Genesis. The former stories are much older than the latter at a literary level, but it may be that both represent oral traditions going back to a real event. The biblical story may have been written up in response to the Mesopotamian version in order to 'correct' its theology.

- In Genesis there is only one God; all the power belongs to Him rather than being shared out among a number of gods in the pantheon.
- In Genesis, God is still personal; some of His thoughts and feelings are described. But the weakness and capriciousness of the Babylonian gods do not appear. He is not fearful, ignorant, greedy, or jealous; He is not annoyed by human rowdiness, but grieved by human corruption (6:6). Noah is saved, not because he is some god's favourite, but because he is righteous and blameless – God is just.
- In the Babylonian story, the flood, once started, was beyond Enlil's control. In the Bible, the Flood is totally under God's control.
- Utnapishtim is a great hero and apparently a king, a major character who is very talkative and active, even shutting himself into his ship. On the other hand, Noah is an ordinary man who never speaks, and is said repeatedly to obey God.

Noah's two initiatives in the story, apart from compliance with explicit commands, are to send out birds to test the state of the drying world, and to offer sacrifice. He thus typifies righteousness in terms of obedience, alertness to the state of the world around, and acknowledgment of dependence upon God.

God reissues the original creation blessing upon the survivors of the Flood, yet shifts significantly the relationship between humanity and the animals. Later visions of God's restored earth revert to the earlier more harmonious scenario (see Isa. 11:6–9). The prohibition against eating blood finds expression in later laws (eg Lev. 7:26–27); blood is identified with life, of which a beating heart and a strong pulse are the clearest evidence. Such prohibitions expressed respect for life, and thus for the giver of life.

An important principle is found in Genesis 9:6, and is often quoted in debates about the death penalty. We have already seen that God's response to Abel's murder includes the prohibition of vengeance on Cain – so that simple quotation of proof texts is inadequate interpretation of the way God speaks through the Bible. Christian debates about capital punishment must be placed in the framework of Jesus' teaching and death that recapture God's creation intentions (cf His teaching on marriage in Matthew 19:4–9) – see the section Seeing Jesus in the Scriptures.

The notion of covenant is of great significance in the Bible. Here we notice its unconditional aspect – knowing human tendencies only too well, God yet commits Himself to His world, knowing what this must continually cost Him. Later covenants are made with Israel (especially Abraham, Moses and David), and renewed as prophesied through the Messiah. Thus the covenant in Jesus' blood extends God's promise to the world even more profoundly than did that with Noah.

Conclude with prayer.

Week Seven: Disrespect and Confusion

Aims:
- To bring this group activity to a good ending.
- To explore two short stories that show human sinfulness continues after the Flood, raising the question of what new initiative God might employ.
- To glimpse this initiative in the beginning of the second half of the book of Genesis.

Disrespect
In these chapters we have observed typical family problems; dissension between husband and wife (Gen. 3) and dissension between siblings (Gen. 4); here we encounter dissension between parent and child.

How Noah discovered what Ham had done is not related (perhaps Noah inquired about being covered by the strange garment). It is not clear why Ham is identified as 'the youngest son' when he has previously been mentioned second after Shem, neither is it explained why Canaan, son of Ham (9:18), should be cursed rather than his father (perhaps because God had recently pronounced a blessing on Noah's sons, 9:1).

In Israel's story the Canaanites were regularly despised as engaging in idolatry and abominable practices, and these curses may be understood as providing a rationale for their degraded reputation.

Confusion
Since the eighteenth-century, Western culture has harboured the myth of progress, an overconfidence in the potential for human achievement for example: science will unlock the

mysteries of the universe; medicine will eliminate disease and death; education will lift the race from darkness and sin; trade will alleviate poverty. From time to time this myth has been shaken, especially by the First World War, and more recently by environmental concerns, but it often reappears after a few years.

Genesis 11 and the Tower of Babel challenges this myth of progress. Human beings cannot construct their own way of transcending the limitations of human existence. Christianity does not offer a utopian vision of a perfected society, but calls people to serve Christ in the kingdom of God. The Church has a message to individuals burdened by expectations of human perfection and unrealistic drives for control. But it must also challenge society's (or politicians') frequent overconfidence in technology, wonder drugs, 'freedom and democracy' and military intervention.

A preview

The family relationships are set out briefly, including the unlooked-for death of the eldest son, Haran, and the barrenness (emphasised) of Abram's wife, Sarai. Having lived in Ur of the Chaldeans in southern Mesopotamia, Terah set out on a long journey to Canaan with Abram, Sarai and Lot (Nahor and Milcah are not mentioned, though they also may have been in the party). However, they settled for a time at Haran, about halfway to Canaan, and there the old man died.

In the Introduction to this guide it was argued that the literary structure of Genesis indicates that chapters 1–11 must be read in conjunction with chapters 12–50. So this study guide draws to a close by suggesting participants discuss how God's famous speech to Abraham connects with the early chapters of Genesis. Certain themes are transposed into a new key, such as:

- The blessing pronounced on the human race in 1:28; 9:1 is re-expressed to one particular man, Abraham, and his descendants.
- The motive of the tower builders, making a great name (11:4), is turned around in God's third promise to Abraham.
- The conflictual nature of life (3:14–15; 3:17–19; 4:11) is recognised in the cursing element (sixth promise).
- The goal of blessing for all peoples on earth forms an important answer to the questions raised by chapters 1–11.

In conclusion, the group should reflect on anything about these studies that has been particularly striking, and use these in a final time of prayer.

Selected books in print recommended for further study

T. Desmond Alexander and David W. Baker (eds), *Dictionary of the Old Testament Pentateuch* (Downers Grove, IL: InterVarsity, 2003).

Mark E. Biddle, *Missing the Mark: Sin and Its Consequences in Biblical Theology* (Nashville, TN: Abingdon, 2005).

Terence E. Fretheim, *God and World in the Old Testament: A Relational Theology of Creation* (Nashville, TN: Abingdon, 2005).

Tremper Longman III, *How to Read Genesis* (Downers Grove, IL: InterVarsity, 2005).

J. Richard Middleton, *The Liberating Image: the Imago Dei in Genesis 1* (Grand Rapids, MI: Brazos, 2005).

Gordon Wenham, *Genesis 1–15* Word Biblical Commentary (Waco, TX: Word, 1987).

The *Cover to Cover* Bible Study Series

1 Corinthians
Growing a Spirit-filled church
ISBN: 978-1-85345-374-8

2 Corinthians
Restoring harmony
ISBN: 978-1-85345-551-3

1,2,3 John
Walking in the truth
ISBN: 978-1-78259-763-6

1 Peter
Good reasons for hope
ISBN: 978-1-78259-088-0

2 Peter
Living in the light of God's
promises
ISBN: 978-1-78259-403-1

23rd Psalm
The Lord is my shepherd
ISBN: 978-1-85345-449-3

1 Timothy
Healthy churches – effective
Christians
ISBN: 978-1-85345-291-8

2 Timothy and Titus
Vital Christianity
ISBN: 978-1-85345-338-0

Abraham
Adventures of faith
ISBN: 978-1-78259-089-7

Acts 1–12
Church on the move
ISBN: 978-1-85345-574-2

Acts 13–28
To the ends of the earth
ISBN: 978-1-85345-592-6

Barnabas
Son of encouragement
ISBN: 978-1-85345-911-5

Bible Genres
Hearing what the Bible really says
ISBN: 978-1-85345-987-0

Daniel
Living boldly for God
ISBN: 978-1-85345-986-3

David
A man after God's own heart
ISBN: 978-1-78259-444-4

Ecclesiastes
Hard questions and spiritual
answers
ISBN: 978-1-85345-371-7

Elijah
A man and his God
ISBN: 978-1-85345-575-9

Elisha
A lesson in faithfulness
ISBN: 978-1-78259-494-9

Ephesians
Claiming your inheritance
ISBN: 978-1-85345-229-1

Esther
For such a time as this
ISBN: 978-1-85345-511-7

Ezekiel
A prophet for all times
ISBN: 978-1-78259-836-7

Fruit of the Spirit
Growing more like Jesus
ISBN: 978-1-85345-375-5

Galatians
Freedom in Christ
ISBN: 978-1-85345-648-0

Genesis 1–11
Foundations of reality
ISBN: 978-1-85345-404-2

Genesis 12–50
Founding fathers of faith
ISBN: 978-1-78259-960-9

God's Rescue Plan
Finding God's fingerprints on
human history
ISBN: 978-1-85345-294-9

Great Prayers of the Bible
Applying them to our lives toda
ISBN: 978-1-85345-253-6

Habakkuk
Choosing God's way
ISBN: 978-1-78259-843-5

Haggai
Motivating God's people
ISBN: 978-1-78259-686-8

Hebrews
Jesus – simply the best
ISBN: 978-1-85345-337-3

Isaiah 1–39
Prophet to the nations
ISBN: 978-1-85345-510-0

Isaiah 40–66
Prophet of restoration
ISBN: 978-1-85345-550-6

Jacob
Taking hold of God's blessing
ISBN: 978-1-78259-685-1

James
Faith in action
ISBN: 978-1-85345-293-2

Jeremiah
The passionate prophet
ISBN: 978-1-85345-372-4

John's Gospel
Exploring the seven miraculous signs
ISBN: 978-1-85345-295-6

Jonah
Rescued from the depths
ISBN: 978-1-78259-762-9

Joseph
The power of forgiveness and reconciliation
ISBN: 978-1-85345-252-9

Joshua 1-10
Hand in hand with God
ISBN: 978-1-85345-542-7

Judges 1-8
The spiral of faith
ISBN: 978-1-85345-681-7

Judges 9-21
Learning to live God's way
ISBN: 978-1-85345-910-8

Luke
A prescription for living
ISBN: 978-1-78259-270-9

Mark
Life as it is meant to be lived
ISBN: 978-1-85345-233-8

Mary
The mother of Jesus
ISBN: 978-1-78259-402-4

Moses
Face to face with God
ISBN: 978-1-85345-336-6

Names of God
Exploring the depths of God's character
ISBN: 978-1-85345-680-0

Nehemiah
Principles for life
ISBN: 978-1-85345-335-9

Parables
Communicating God on earth
ISBN: 978-1-85345-340-3

Philemon
From slavery to freedom
ISBN: 978-1-85345-453-0

Philippians
Living for the sake of the gospel
ISBN: 978-1-85345-421-9

Prayers of Jesus
Hearing His heartbeat
ISBN: 978-1-85345-647-3

Proverbs
Living a life of wisdom
ISBN: 978-1-85345-373-1

Revelation 1-3
Christ's call to the Church
ISBN: 978-1-85345-461-5

Revelation 4-22
The Lamb wins! Christ's final victory
ISBN: 978-1-85345-411-0

Rivers of Justice
Responding to God's call to righteousness today
ISBN: 978-1-85345-339-7

Ruth
Loving kindness in action
ISBN: 978-1-85345-231-4

The Armour of God
Living in His strength
ISBN: 978-1-78259-583-0

The Beatitudes
Immersed in the grace of Christ
ISBN: 978-1-78259-495-6

The Creed
Belief in action
ISBN: 978-1-78259-202-0

The Divine Blueprint
God's extraordinary power in ordinary lives
ISBN: 978-1-85345-292-5

The Holy Spirit
Understanding and experiencing Him
ISBN: 978-1-85345-254-3

The Image of God
His attributes and character
ISBN: 978-1-85345-228-4

The Kingdom
Studies from Matthew's Gospel
ISBN: 978-1-85345-251-2

The Letter to the Colossians
In Christ alone
ISBN: 978-1-855345-405-9

The Letter to the Romans
Good news for everyone
ISBN: 978-1-85345-250-5

The Lord's Prayer
Praying Jesus' way
ISBN: 978-1-85345-460-8

The Prodigal Son
Amazing grace
ISBN: 978-1-85345-412-7

The Second Coming
Living in the light of Jesus' return
ISBN: 978-1-85345-422-6

The Sermon on the Mount
Life within the new covenant
ISBN: 978-1-85345-370-0

Thessalonians
Building Church in changing times
ISBN: 978-1-78259-443-7

The Ten Commandments
Living God's Way
ISBN: 978-1-85345-593-3

The Uniqueness of our Faith
What makes Christianity distinctive?
ISBN: 978-1-85345-232-1

For current prices or to order, visit **cwr.org.uk/shop**
Available online or from Christian bookshops.

Be inspired by God.
Every day.

Confidently face life's challenges by equipping yourself daily with God's Word. There is something for everyone...

Every Day with Jesus

Selwyn Hughes' renowned writing is updated by Mick Brooks into these trusted and popular notes.

Life Every Day

Jeff Lucas helps apply the Bible to life through his trademark humour and insight.

Inspiring Women Every Day

Encouragement, uplifting scriptures and insightful daily thoughts for women.

The Manual

A straight-talking guide to help men walk with God. Written by Carl Beech.

To find out more about all our daily Bible reading notes, or to take out a subscription, visit **cwr.org.uk/biblenotes** or call 01252 784700.
Also available in Christian bookshops.

 Printed format Large print format Email format 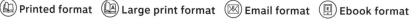 Ebook format

SmallGroup central

All of our small group ideas and resources in one place

Online:

smallgroupcentral.org.uk
is filled with free video teaching, tools, articles and a whole host of ideas.

On the road:

A range of seminars themed for small groups can be brought to your local community. Contact us at **hello@smallgroupcentral.org.uk**

In print:

Books, study guides and DVDs covering an extensive list of themes, Bible books and life issues.

Find out more at:
smallgroupcentral.org.uk

Courses and events

Waverley Abbey College

Publishing and media

Conference facilities

Transforming lives

CWR's vision is to enable people to experience personal transformation through applying God's Word to their lives and relationships.

Our Bible-based training and resources help people around the world to:
• Grow in their walk with God
• Understand and apply Scripture to their lives
• Resource themselves and their church
• Develop pastoral care and counselling skills
• Train for leadership
• Strengthen relationships, marriage and family life and much more.

Our insightful writers provide daily Bible reading notes and other resources for all ages, and our experienced course designers and presenters have gained an international reputation for excellence and effectiveness.

CWR's Training and Conference Centre in Surrey, England, provides excellent facilities in an idyllic setting – ideal for both learning and spiritual refreshment.

CWR Applying God's Word
to everyday life and relationships

CWR, Waverley Abbey House,
Waverley Lane, Farnham,
Surrey GU9 8EP, UK

Telephone: **+44 (0)1252 784700**
Email: **info@cwr.org.uk**
Website: **www.cwr.org.uk**

Registered Charity No. 294387
Company Registration No. 1990308

THE POCKET BOOK OF

GARDEN
EXPERIMENTS

BLOOMSBURY WILDLIFE
Bloomsbury Publishing Plc
50 Bedford Square, London, WC1B 3DP, UK

BLOOMSBURY, BLOOMSBURY WILDLIFE
and the Diana logo are trademarks of Bloomsbury Publishing Plc.

First published in Great Britain 2020 in association with the Royal Horticultural Society

A catalogue record for this book is available from the British Library

ISBN: HB: 978-1-4729-7630-7; ePub: 978-1-4729-7629-1; ePDF: 978-1-4729-7631-4

2 4 6 8 10 9 7 5 3 1

Design by Lindsey Johns, illustrations by Sarah Skeate, project management by Kate Duffy
RHS Publisher – Rae Spencer-Jones
RHS Editor – Simon Maughan
RHS Head of Editorial – Chris Young

Printed and bound in China by
Regent Publishing Services

Bloomsbury Publishing Plc makes every effort to ensure that the papers used in the
manufacture of our books are natural, recyclable products made from wood grown in
well-managed forests. Our manufacturing processes conform to the environmental
regulations of the country of origin.

To find out more about our authors and books visit www.bloomsbury.com
and sign up for our newsletters

The Royal Horticultural Society is the UK's leading gardening charity. We aim to enrich
everyone's life through plants, and make the UK a greener and more beautiful place. This
vision underpins all that we do – from inspirational gardens and shows, through our scientific
research, to our education and community programmes. We are committed to inspiring
everyone to grow. We share our knowledge through books, websites, podcasts and magazines,
hold world-class collections of horticultural books and botanical art, and sell the very best
plants and gardening gifts. For more information visit rhs.org.uk or call 020 3176 5800.

THE POCKET BOOK OF

GARDEN
EXPERIMENTS

80
FUN ACTIVITIES
FOR FAMILIES

HELEN PILCHER

BLOOMSBURY WILDLIFE
LONDON • OXFORD • NEW YORK • NEW DELHI • SYDNEY

CONTENTS

WONDERFUL WILDLIFE
8

SOIL SCIENCE
64

3

FASCINATING
FLORA
90

4

KITCHEN SINK
SCIENCE
146

INTRODUCTION

If you've ever asked a question or wondered why something is the way it is, then you are a scientist. Scientists are interested in how the world works. They are inquisitive. They ask lots of questions. They make predictions or 'hypotheses', and then design experiments to test if their hypotheses are true. As new results come in, scientists are constantly revising what they think about the world.

This book is designed to bring out your inner scientist. It will help you to appreciate the natural world and the wonders that live in it. It's packed full of experiments and activities that will stretch your imagination and foster your natural curiosity.

All of the activities are centred around the garden. They can either be carried out in the garden, or use

items that come from the garden. If you don't have a garden, don't worry. Head to a local park or a wild green space instead. Some of the activities can be done in small spaces, like a balcony, window box or plant pot, and some can be done indoors. All of them derive their inspiration from the natural world and the fascinating things that live in it.

Many of the experiments can safely be carried out without adult interference. Sometimes, however, adult assistance is recommended and, where this is the case, it is clearly marked at the start of the experiment. The activities in this book are designed for young people aged 11 or above, but younger kids will also enjoy them – they may just need a little more help.

The book is split into four different sections: wonderful wildlife, soil science, fascinating flora and kitchen sink science. You can work through them in order, or dip in and out of the different sections when something catches your eye.

The ingredients for each activity are clearly listed. Most of these are simple items that can be readily found in the garden and the home.

The instructions are clear and concise, and there are fun facts scattered through the book. Did you know, for example, that butterflies taste with their feet?

So, what are you waiting for? Get digging, planting, growing, making, spotting, designing, decorating and experimenting. But most of all, get in your garden and have some fun!

WONDERFUL
WILDLIFE

It doesn't matter if you live in the
middle of a big city or on a farm in the middle
of the countryside – wildlife is everywhere.
The earth is buzzing with things that fly,
swim, crawl, hop and run. All too often
we overlook the creatures that live on our
doorstep, but if you take the time to stop,
look and listen, you'll realise just how busy
your garden really is.

WONDERFUL WILDLIFE

Pollinators like bees and butterflies (see the Peacock Butterfly opposite) visit the blooms in our patio planters and flowerbeds. Amphibians hide in moist, dark places. Birds belt out tunes from high in the trees, and swoop down to nibble the treats in the bird feeders we hang up. Minibeasts, like snails, spiders and beetles, patrol the borders, whilst caterpillars cling to their food plants and munch away quietly.

If you're lucky enough to have a pond, it will be teeming with life. Ponds are wildlife magnets. They're a draw to water-living creatures, like pond skaters, freshwater shrimps as well as frogs and damselflies (see below), and land-living animals like birds and some mammals, which come to drink from their edges.

It's great to look at and wonderful to study, but beyond that, the wildlife in our garden plays a vital role. Every creature is part of an interconnected web of living things and their habitats, and they all have a role to play. By transferring pollen, pollinators help plants to reproduce. Birds help to keep the insect population in check. Caterpillars provide food for birds, and snails help to consume rotting plants and leaves.

It's time to celebrate the wildlife in your garden, and learn a little more about it. The experiments and activities in this section of the book are designed to make you take notice of the wildlife that surrounds you. There are experiments to help you attract and record wildlife, and understand the needs that different living things have.

Along the way, you'll learn how to give the wildlife in your garden a helping hand, by putting out food and creating new habitats for wildlife to thrive. You'll be making homes for hoverflies, painting treacle on tree trunks and collecting caterpillars in an umbrella.

Best of all, once you start noticing and caring for the wildlife in your garden, you'll never stop. It doesn't take much to make your garden a wilder place, and welcoming wildlife is one of the most rewarding things you can do.

MAKE A
SCIENCE JOURNAL

Scientists always write up their experiments so they have a permanent record of what they have learned. Create your own science journal so you can keep notes of all the activities you try from this book.

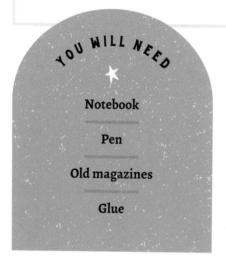

YOU WILL NEED

★

Notebook

Pen

Old magazines

Glue

★ To make a science journal, find an unused notebook. One with a hardback is good because it's easier to write in when you're out and about. If you don't have a notebook, you can staple some blank pieces of paper together.

★ Write your name on the front cover and label the notebook 'Science Journal'. Decorate it with doodles or cut out pictures from magazines and stick them on. Plants, animals and landscapes would all look good, but this is your journal. Decorate it however you like.

★ Record every experiment and activity that you do. Start each one on a new page. Scientists always write up their experiments in a particular way, so this a good model to follow:

★ First, write the date and the title at the top of the page, and then a brief description of what you are going to do. This will be the Introduction section. For example:

MARK AND RECAPTURE SNAILS
An experiment to determine how many snails are living in a corner of the garden.

List all the items you are going to use, then write step-by-step instructions describing how you are going to do it. That way, if you ever need to repeat the experiment (good scientists do this a lot) you'll know exactly what to do. This is the Methods section.

When you've finished your experiment or activity, write up the results. If you've made observations or collected data, write it down. If you've built something, draw a diagram of it or take a photo and stick it in. This is the Results section.

Write up each experiment or activity in four sections with four different headings: Introduction, Methods, Results, and Discussion.

Now write down what you have learned. How successful was the activity? Did the thing you were building work as you'd hoped? How could it be improved? What can you learn from the results of your experiment? Look at the information that you've gathered, and draw a conclusion. This is the Discussion section.

BIRDSONG PLAYLIST

People often walk around wearing headphones, but when we're busy listening to music, we're missing out on one of the best sounds around: birdsong. Make a playlist of the bird songs that you hear, and learn to recognise the calls of your favourite birds.

YOU WILL NEED

★

A recording device, like a smartphone

A pair of ears

★ The best time to record birdsong is during the day when there are fewer birds singing and less background noise. Using your recording device, start by recording five different bird songs. See if you can spot the birds that are making these noises. It's often easier to recognise a bird by sight than it is by sound, so this helps to match the bird to the song.

★ Different bird species sing different songs. Some belt out big melodies, whilst others sing more softly. Some of the tunes are long and complex, whilst others are short and simple. When you first start learning, it can be difficult to tell these different songs apart, so it's a good idea to record them and play them back.

★ When you are at home, try to identify the remaining songs. There are lots of online resources that can help with this. Concentrate on the structure of the song. Are there unusual features or parts that are repeated? Some songs contain recognisable sections that are unique to particular species.

Learning to identify birdsong is like learning a new language. The more you practise, the easier it gets. Label the songs you have identified and listen to them over and over. You can wear your headphones for this bit! If you like you can re-order the tunes to create your very own birdsong playlist.

As you become familiar with different bird songs, you can start to record where and when you hear them. Make a note of these observations in your science journal.

Birds make a remarkable variety of different noises. Birds can hiss, wheeze, growl and boom.

Birds sing for lots of different reasons, such as to attract a mate or defend their territory. Sometimes they change the sounds that they make. Some birds, for example, make high-pitched alarm calls to warn others that there are predators around. Try to recognise and record some of these more unusual calls. Do you notice any patterns emerging? Are some songs heard more often in particular places? If they are, you may have stumbled upon a bird that is defending its patch.

BIG BIRD COUNT

Scientists think that more than one in ten bird species are in danger of going extinct. Even common species are becoming rarer. Keep a record of the birds in your neighbourhood by counting them to see how they are doing.

Find somewhere comfy to watch the birds. If you have a garden where birds visit, you could choose to watch them through a window. Alternatively, find a chair to take outside and then settle down in a good spot. If you don't have a garden, head to a park or a wild green space. Many birds live in cities, so if you find yourself surrounded by buildings, that's fine too. Just have a look and see what you can spot.

Sit quietly and don't make any sudden movements. Relax, have a drink and a snack, and watch the birds for an hour. Using your bird guide, make a note of all the different species that you see. Use obvious features, like the bird's size, shape and colouring, to help identify what they are.

Binoculars
(if you have a pair)

Bird guide

Pen and paper

A drink and
a snack

Record your data because you never know when it will be useful.
Some universities and wildlife charities run citizen science projects
where they encourage members of the public to record their bird sightings
and send them in. This is a great idea because it helps scientists
to understand how bird populations are changing, and how we can
all help to save endangered birds.

As well as making a note of the species, record the number of individual birds that you see. Make a note of the maximum number of each species that you see at any one time. So, if you see a group of two sparrows together, and then later on a cluster of four sparrows, the number to write down is four. This means you are less likely to double-count the same birds.

Keep going back to your spot, and see how the bird life changes over time. Some species, for example, are more numerous in the spring and summer because that is when they breed. Sometimes new species of birds appear and then disappear. These could be migratory species that have travelled vast distances. Their numbers may change across the day. Some species, for instance, are more active during the day and others are more active at night.

INSECT UMBRELLA

There are more than 150,000 species of butterflies and moths. Their caterpillars have evolved to feed on many different food plants. Determine the food preferences of tree-dwelling caterpillars with this simple insect umbrella experiment.

⭐ Most moths and butterflies lay their eggs when the weather warms up. The eggs hatch into caterpillars, so if you want to find them, this is an activity for a warm spring or summer day.

⭐ Head into a garden, park or wild space and look for a deciduous tree with low-hanging branches. Deciduous trees are the ones that lose their leaves in winter. Insects find their leaves delicious! Avoid trees that are evergreen. Evergreen trees keep their leaves all year round. They tend to have glossy, waxy leaves that caterpillars don't like.

⭐ Once you have found your tree, start by looking at its leaves. If they look nibbled or have tiny holes in them, then something has been snacking on them. If the holes look fresh, the insect could be nearby. See if you can find some of these insects and identify them.

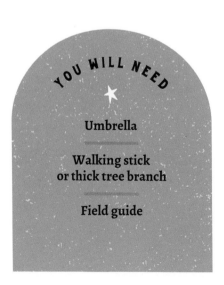

YOU WILL NEED
★

Umbrella

**Walking stick
or thick tree branch**

Field guide

Next, look for a slender branch that is at roughly head height. Open the umbrella and turn it upside down, so the spokes and the handle are pointing up to the sky. Then put it on the ground underneath the branch.

Now take your stick and hit the branch. Give it a few short, sharp taps. Any caterpillars that are clinging to the leaves should fall into the upside-down umbrella. Take care not to damage the tree. Don't hit the leaves or any fresh shoots, as you may harm them.

Have a look at what you've got. Count the different varieties and identify what you have collected using a field guide. Then turn the umbrella over and let the insects go nearby. Now try again with a

different type of tree. Are the sorts of insect that you find the same or different? Make a list of the caterpillars that you find on the various different food plants.

Some caterpillars are specialist feeders that only eat one type of plant. Others are generalists that have evolved to eat a variety of different plants. Which are more common in your garden?

SWEET TREATS FOR MOTHS

Many people think that moths are boring and brown, but the truth is very different. Moths are often brightly coloured, come in many different shapes and sizes, and play an important role in the natural world. You can attract them using this sweet moth treat.

YOU WILL NEED

Bottle of cola 330ml (11fl oz)

500g (17oz) dark brown sugar

200g (7oz) black treacle

Large saucepan

Decorator's brush

Torch

Field guide

★ This experiment works best during the summer. Although some moths fly during the day, most come out at night. Some of these are attracted to sugary solutions because they are similar to the nectar and sap that the moths usually feed on.

★ Prepare your sugary solution. Ask an adult to help you heat up the cola in a large saucepan. Let the liquid boil then turn the heat down and let it bubble gently for 5 minutes. Whilst it is simmering, add the sugar, one spoonful at a time. Keep stirring the liquid. When the sugar has dissolved, pour in the treacle. Then let it bubble for a few more minutes. Finally, take the saucepan off the heat and set it to one side. Leave the mixture for a couple of hours, so it cools thoroughly.

At dusk, head outside with your mixture and your brush, and look for a place with lots of leafy, green trees. A garden or a park will do. Dip the brush into the mixture and paint it on to ten different tree trunks at eye-level height. Apply the mixture generously, creating big sticky patches on the tree bark. Warning – this can get messy! Then go home and wash your hands.

An hour or so later, when it is properly dark, go out and check the tree trunks. Shine the torch on the freshly painted bark. Photograph or draw what you find and add the pictures to your journal. Try to identify some of the species using a field guide, then repeat the experiment a few weeks later. Different moths visit the garden at different times of year, so what do you find now? Don't worry about cleaning up. Next time it rains, the mixture will wash off.

BUG HOTELS

There are lots of bugs and creepy-crawlies that are good for the garden, but sometimes they struggle to find anywhere to live. It helps if the garden is not too tidy, but you can also build a deluxe bug hotel out of recycled materials and watch the creepy-crawlies move in.

YOU WILL NEED

Some building materials such as:

Old pieces of wood

Straw, moss, dry leaves

Old terracotta pots, or roof tiles, bricks

Logs, pine cones, bamboo canes

Bark, woodchips, sand or soil

Cardboard tubes, or corrugated cardboard

Roofing felt, if available

First, think about where to put your bug hotel. You need a flat space to put it on, and a sheltered spot would be good. Different insects will move in depending on whether it's sunny or shady, so you may decide to make two small hotels rather than one big one.

Start by making a sturdy structure. Think about how to best use your materials to make a hotel with several 'floors'. Flat sheets of wood, supported on bricks, are an easy option.

Remember to put a roof on the top to keep out the rain. If you have roofing felt then fix that on as the top layer. You may need a hammer and nails, and an adult to help. Old roof tiles are another option.

Once you've built the outside of your hotel, it's time for some interior decorating! The idea is to create as many different nooks and crannies as you can, using different materials, to attract different bugs. You could stuff a section with straw or dry leaves, or cram it full of hollow stems like bamboo canes. Can you fill a cardboard tube with moss, or roll up corrugated cardboard nice and tight? Some bugs like to burrow, so try filling an old plant pot with sand or soil and see what moves in.

You can make a very simple bug hotel by filling a terracotta plant pot with short sections of hollow stems (like bamboo). Lay it on its side somewhere that is sunny but sheltered, and wait for the bugs to arrive.

It will take a while for the first guests to arrive, but keep checking so that you can see what is living in your hotel. Can you name all of the bugs and creepy-crawlies? Maybe you could draw pictures of them and keep them in a guestbook for your bug hotel.

MINI MAMMAL PRINTS

Record some of the small animals that visit your garden by capturing their footprints in this mini mammal tunnel.

Wash and dry the juice cartons, then cut the top and bottoms off to make three long rectangular tubes. Slide the three tubes together to make one long tunnel. Now tape the tubes together.

Line the bottom of the tunnel with a long thin sheet of clean white paper. Tape it in place.

Check that the margarine lid will fit inside the tunnel. Now take it out and cut a piece of sponge so that it fits neatly inside the upturned lid.

Moisten the sponge with water and add a good dash of food colouring. When you press your finger into the sponge, the food colouring should stain your skin. If it's too faint, add a bit more colouring.

Fill the bottle top with peanut butter. You can use different types of bait, like cheese or dog food, but peanut butter is good because it's sticky and prolongs the amount of time the mammal will spend standing in the food dye.

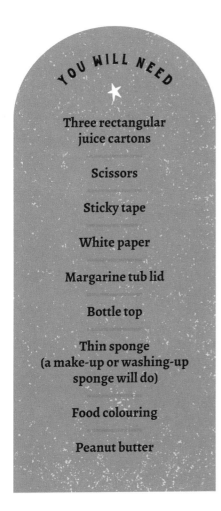

YOU WILL NEED

★

Three rectangular
juice cartons

Scissors

Sticky tape

White paper

Margarine tub lid

Bottle top

Thin sponge
(a make-up or washing-up
sponge will do)

Food colouring

Peanut butter

DID YOU KNOW?
The front paws of mice have
four toes, and their back feet
have five toes. Rat trails are
similar to mouse trails, but the
footprints are larger.

✷ Leave your tunnel for a few days. Check it every morning. Remove the margarine lid and look at the paper. If there's been a visitor, the footprints should be clearly visible on the paper. If you're lucky you may even see a tail print too! Stick the paper in your journal and see if you can identify the footprints. Make a list of all the different species you record.

✷ Now try setting the trap in a wild space, like a woodland. (Check first to see if you need permission.) There will be new species here. What do you find?

✷ Place the bottle top onto the sponge, and slide the margarine lid into the middle of the tunnel. Now carefully carry your construction into the garden. Rodents like to scurry along the sides of walls and fences, so place the tunnel next to a brick wall or garden fence. Camouflage the tunnel by covering it with leaves and branches.

GROW PLANTS FOR WILDLIFE

Plants provide a source of food and shelter for all sorts of animals, like insects and birds. Make your garden more wildlife-friendly by adding a few well-chosen plants, then record the guests that come and visit.

Flowering plants are really important because they provide nectar and pollen for bees and other pollinators. Try to grow lots of different flowers. Go for simple plants with open flowers and single petals. Fussy flowers with multiple layers of petals may look pretty, but they often have less nectar and pollen.

Plants are the basis of all food chains. The more different plants you can grow, the more different kinds of wildlife you will attract to your garden.

Choose flowers that blossom at different times of the year, so you help the insects for as long as possible. Some insects like to stock up on food before they overwinter.

Flowers are nice to have but don't forget about food plants. Many caterpillars and other insects graze on the leaves and stems of smaller plants, shrubs and trees. Grow native plants because they are more likely to attract local insects than unfamiliar plants from far away.

As summer turns to autumn, some birds and mammals eat the seeds and berries produced by some plants. Berries often contain a lot of fat, which helps to build the animals up before the arrival of winter, when there is less food around. Grow a mix of seed-bearing flowers, shrubs and trees.

When you sow your seeds or dig in your plants, make sure you water them well. Then keep an eye out for them. New plants need a lot of watering whilst their roots get established.

If you have a garden, persuade your parents to let it get a bit messy. Fallen leaves help to fertilise the soil, and they provide a home for minibeasts like worms and beetles. Tangled climbers and bushy thickets provide a place for birds to build their nests.

Make a chart in your journal of the animals that visit the plants you have provided. Make a note of the date they visited and the plants that they used. Which is the best plant for wildlife?

BIRD BUFFET

It's always fun to watch birds feeding at a bird table or feeder, but have you ever wondered which snacks are their favourites? You can make a bird buffet and do an experiment to find out.

Lots of people like to leave food out for the birds. This is especially helpful in the winter when natural food is scarce, but it's also useful in spring and summer when parents are bringing up their young. In fact, if you feed the birds, it's a good idea to leave food out all year round.

Just like us, different birds like to eat different things. You can test their preferences by leaving out a variety of different bird foods. Mixed birdseed, sunflower seeds, peanuts and mealworms are good foods to try, but you could also test them on other things like banana or grated mild cheese.

Choose the location for your feeding experiment. It should be somewhere safe, where the birds won't get ambushed by cats or other predators. Bird tables are good because they're high off the ground, but you could also set up the experiment on a balcony or brick wall.

 Now lay out your bird buffet. Put down a handful of each food type. Leave a good space between each pile so the foods don't get mixed up.

 If you want, you can set up the experiment using bird feeders. Fill different feeders with different ingredients and hang them up next to each other.

 Now sit back and watch what happens. Don't be put off if the birds don't come immediately. Birds are often wary of unfamiliar situations, but once they realise the experiment is delicious and safe, they'll keep coming back!

 Set up a chart with columns for the different bird foods, then add in the different species that eat them. Can you spot any patterns? Birds definitely have favourites. What do your birds enjoy the most? Now see if you can find something that they like to eat even more!

DID YOU KNOW?
British great tits are evolving longer beaks than their European counterparts. Scientists think this is because British people love to feed the birds, and the birds' beaks are adapting to the feeders.

HOVERFLY HAVEN

Although hoverflies look a bit like bees and wasps, they are not closely related. You can welcome these harmless pollinators into your garden by building a hoverfly haven.

As their name suggests, hoverflies can often be seen hovering above colourful flowers. Hoverfly larvae are the gardener's friend as they often eat aphids and other troublesome pests. Many hoverflies are mimics. They have evolved to look like bees and wasps, but don't worry – they don't sting at all. This is a disguise that helps to protect them from predators.

DID YOU KNOW?
Hoverflies are thought to be the second most important group of pollinators after wild bees.

There are lots of different kinds of hoverfly. Some lay their eggs on plants, but some breed in still pools of water where their larvae eat decaying plant and animal matter.

Half-fill the ice cream tub with grass cuttings then pour in some water. Add enough water to cover the grass.

Next, add a generous handful of leaves. The leaves will rest on the surface of the water. This gives the female hoverflies somewhere to land when they come to lay their eggs.

Now add the sticks. The sticks need to poke out of the water. You can achieve this by sliding them into the grassy water and then leaning the sticks against the side of the ice cream tub.

Once the eggs have hatched, the larvae will live in the water. The larvae of some hoverfly species breathe underwater by poking a hollow tail-like tube out of the water – just like a snorkel! After turning into pupae, the adult hoverflies emerge. The sticks help them to climb out of the water, and give them a place to flex their wings before taking off.

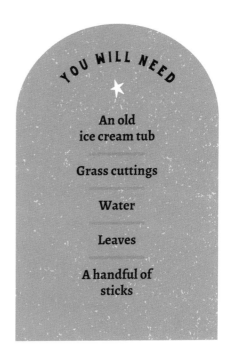

Check your hoverfly haven regularly. In warm weather, the water will evaporate, so keep topping it up. As the grass and leaves begin to break down, it will create the perfect conditions for your very own hoverfly nursery.

Photograph the hoverflies that you find around the haven. There are thousands of different species of hoverflies. Using an online guide, try to identify them. Stick the photos into your journal, and see if you can work out which is the most common species in your patch.

11

ANT FARM

Ants are very industrious. They live in colonies
and work together, helping to keep the environment
clean by decomposing plant and animal matter.
Record how long it takes for ants to create their home
by making an ant farm in a jar.

YOU WILL NEED

★

**Big glass jar
with a lid**

**Small glass jar
with a lid (that fits
inside the big jar)**

**A spare jar (any size)
with a lid**

**Soil from the garden
and water**

An apple

Ants

★ Take the labels off the jars, then
wash and dry them thoroughly.
With its lid on, place the smaller jar
inside the bigger jar. Make it as
central as possible. Start filling the
big jar with dryish soil from the
garden. Pour it down the sides of
the big jar so the soil surrounds the
little jar. Don't completely cover

the little jar. Leave the top of it poking out of the soil. Topsoil is good because it doesn't have any big lumps in it and is often quite sandy. This makes it easier for the ants to move around.

Now go outside and find some ants. Choose your ants wisely. Some varieties have a nasty bite, whilst others are harmless. Check with an adult to make sure the ants are suitable.

You will need to set an ant trap. Mush up a slice of apple with some water and put it into the spare jar. Then lay the open jar on its side on the ground and wait for the ants to wander in. They will be attracted to the sugar. You don't need too many ants – ten to twenty is perfect. Then close the lid and carry them to the ant farm.

DID YOU KNOW?
Some ants can lift more than twenty times their own body weight. If an 11-year-old girl were that strong, she would be able to lift a cow!

Tip the ants and mushed apple into the ant farm, then quickly screw the lid on. Don't worry about making air holes. Ants are tiny and don't need much oxygen, so there will be more than enough inside the jar to keep them going.

Place the jar on a shelf or table – anywhere that is not in direct sunlight – and enjoy! The ants will move the soil around and create an amazing network of subterranean tunnels.

The ants will need feeding every few days. Swap the old apple for a new piece, and add a tiny sprinkle of water. Do this outside in case any ants escape.

Record how long it takes for the ants to make their tunnels. Draw a map of the network they create and stick it in your journal.

WHAT DO WOODLICE LIKE?

All living things have a preferred environment or 'niche'. Some like it hot. Some like it cold. Some like it dry. Others prefer it wet. Woodlice are no different. Find out where they like to live using this simple experiment.

★ Woodlice are small crustaceans. They have a hard outer exoskeleton made up of separate segments, and seven pairs of jointed legs. They can be found hiding under outdoor plant pots, stones, rotting logs and leaf litter. Fill your jar with a small amount of soil, and go out and collect twenty woodlice. Use a paintbrush to flick the woodlice onto a piece of paper, then tip them into the jar.

★ Prepare the experiment. First of all, cut a rectangular hole measuring roughly 10cm × 1cm (4in × ½in) into one of the short sides, or 'walls', of the shoebox. The hole should be right at the bottom of the wall, next to the base of the

shoebox. Now, cut a matching hole into the second shoebox. Check that it is the same size as the first hole.

Using some tape, join the two shoeboxes together, so the holes are perfectly matched up. You should now have one very long box with a wall, with a hole through it, in the middle.

Woodlice aren't fussy eaters. They eat rotting plants, fungi and their own faeces, but they don't pee! They get rid of some waste products by excreting a pungent chemical called ammonia through their exoskeleton.

Place dry soil in one side, and wet soil in the other. Now add ten woodlice to each compartment and put the lids back on the shoeboxes. The woodlice will start to move around and may choose to move from one box into the other. Check the woodlice every 15 minutes and record how many there are in each compartment each time you look. Where did the woodlice like to go and how long did it take them?

Now repeat the experiment, but this time, leave the lids off. Did the woodlice still make the same choice? How long did it take them this time? Can you work out how fast they moved?

MAKE A
BUG SUCKER

**Gardens and open spaces are full of tiny bugs
so small that they're difficult to pick up and study.
Fear not! Suck them up with this homemade bug
sucker or 'pooter', and record how many different
types of tiny bug are in your garden.**

Using the hammer and nail, create two holes in the metal lid of the glass jar. Enlarge the holes so the plastic tubing will be able to fit through them. You may need an adult to help with this.

Prepare the tubing. Clear, plastic tubing can be bought from a DIY store. You'll need about 50cm (20in). It should be 7–10mm (¼–³/₈in) wide. Cut the tubing into two pieces, about 15cm (6in) and 35cm (13¹/₂in) long. Poke the tubing through the holes in the lid. There should be about 5cm (2in) of tubing on the inside of the jar once you have put it all together.

Cut a circle from the pair of tights. It should be about 5cm (2in) across. Wrap the stretchy fabric around the end of the shorter tube, then fasten it in place using the elastic band. When the jar is reassembled, this should be on the inside of the jar.

Colour one of the stickers green, and the other one red. Stick the green sticker onto the other end of the short tube. This is the tube you will suck through. Mark the end of the longer tube with the red sticker. This is the nozzle of the sucker.

Make the lid airtight by sticking some putty or plasticine around the joins where the tubes meet the lid. Screw the lid back onto the jar. Your insect sucker is now ready to go!

Go into the garden and find some minibeasts. Aim the nozzle end of the sucker (with the red sticker) at the insect you would like to collect, then give a short, sharp suck on the end of the other tube (with the green sticker). The insect will be hoovered up the nozzle and into the jar. You can now observe it carefully. Don't forget to let them go when you have finished.

How many different types of tiny insect can you find? Draw what you find in your journal. Look in various habitats, like dark, shady places and exposed, sunny flowerbeds. Do you find different insects in other habitats?

TOAD SHACK

Every creature deserves somewhere nice to live, and toads are no exception. See if you can attract them to your garden by building them their very own toad shack.

Paint a colourful design or picture on the plant pot. You could paint something that a toad would like, such as lots of delicious flies.

YOU WILL NEED

Medium
plant pot

Paints and
a brush

Trowel

Leaves

Shallow bowl

Toads are amphibians. They have thin permeable skin. This means that liquids and gases can pass through the skin easily. This is good, because it helps them to breathe – and bad, because they dry out easily. That's why toads like to live in damp, shady places. Choose a location for your toad shack. It should be somewhere shady with lots of plants and places to hide. This will help to keep the toad's skin moist. Flowerbeds and overgrown corners are good spots.

Dig a hole that is big enough for the plant pot to fit in when it's on its side. Don't make it too deep. The top half of the plant pot should be above ground.

Turn the plant pot on its side and place it in the hole. Add a handful of wet leaves so the toad has somewhere nice to sit.

You might think that toads need to live in ponds. Sometimes they do, but they will also be quite happy in the toad shack as long as there is a source of water nearby. Fill the shallow bowl with water and place it near the toad shack.

Be patient. It could take weeks or even months for a toad to move in. Keep checking the shack on a regular basis. You can also look for toads in dark places under logs and leaves. Toads have bumpy, rough skin and frogs have smooth skin that is covered in mucus. When you do

DID YOU KNOW?
Toads catch beetles, spiders and other prey using their long sticky tongues. Unlike human tongues, which are attached at the back of the mouth, toad tongues are attached at the front of the mouth. This is because toads don't chew their food. They just swallow it straight down. Gulp!

find a toad, pick it up carefully and put it in its new home. Now wash your hands. It's up to the toad to decide if it wants to stay.

15

POND DIPPING

Ponds are absolute havens for wildlife.
Beneath the surface of the water, there's a whole
world of weird and wonderful creatures just waiting
to be found. Find out what's lurking in the depths
of your local pond.

YOU WILL NEED

★

Shallow tray
or big ice cream tub

Net
(see pages 160–61
for how to make one)

Field guide

Magnifying glass
(if you have one)

Smartphone with camera
(if you have one)

Science journal

Jam jar

★ Half-fill the tray with water from
the pond and put it to one side on
level ground. Avoid placing the tray
in direct sunlight as this will warm
the water and could harm the
animals that you catch.

★ Dip the net into the pond and
sweep it through the water in a
figure-of-eight shape. This helps
to make sure that anything you
catch will stay in the net.

★ Don't lean too far out. The areas
around the edge of the pond will
have lots of life in them. Be careful
not to scoop up mud or stir up
the sediment at the bottom of the
pond. This will clog up your net
and make it difficult to see what
you have caught.

Empty the net by carefully turning it inside out into the tray. Let the water settle. Take a look at what you have caught, and use your field guide to identify the different creatures. Some of the animals will be very small, so use the magnifying glass to help you. If you're struggling to identify something, take a photo then look it up later. Make a note of all the different creatures that you find in your science journal.

Don't keep the animals in the tray for too long. Once you have finished with them, use the glass jar to scoop them up and return them to the pond. Keep searching. When you have completely finished, tip the contents of the tray back into the pond. Make sure you wash your hands after this activity.

A BIRDBATH
FOR ALL SEASONS

As their natural habitat disappears to make way for towns, cities and agricultural land, birds are becoming increasingly reliant on gardens. Help them by making them a birdbath, then record all the visitors that use it.

YOU WILL NEED

Shallow tray
(a metallic dustbin lid
is ideal)

Three bricks

Water

A big stone and
some gravel

Tea light candles
and matches

Choose your dish. The birdbath will be out in the garden all year round, so it needs to be made of something that won't shatter when it freezes, such as metal or ceramic. A large metal dustbin lid makes an excellent birdbath because it has shallow sloping sides and is nice and wide. Plastic alternatives won't work, because in the winter the birdbath will be heated, and the dish could melt.

Find somewhere flat to put the birdbath. It should be somewhere that is easily visible. Ideally, it should be in a big open space with trees and bushes nearby. This will help the birds keep an eye out for predators whilst they visit the

Birds need fresh water all year round for drinking and bathing. This is especially important in the winter when water freezes, and in the summer when it evaporates more easily.

birdbath. If cats come to your garden, prune back any trees or shrubs that are within pouncing distance. This will make it harder for the cats to ambush the birds.

Lay out three bricks on the ground in a triangular shape with a space in the middle. Balance the dish on the bricks, making sure it is stable. Add a large stone to the middle of the dish, surrounded by a sprinkling

of small stones or gravel. The stones provide a perch for birds to sit on, and a lifeline for any beetles or bugs that fall in – they'll be able to crawl onto the stones, dry themselves and then fly away.

Fill the birdbath with water. It should be no more than 10cm (4in) deep. In the winter, when the temperature drops, place a lighted tea light candle in the middle of the bricks underneath the birdbath. This will help to prevent the water from freezing. Check the birdbath every day, and top up the water as needed.

In your journal, record the different birds that use the bath. Note the date when they visited and what the weather conditions were like. Do the birds use the bath more at certain times of year?

MAKE A BUTTERFLY FEEDER

Butterflies are welcome visitors to any outdoor space. These important pollinators always add a splash of colour. Find out how to encourage them into your garden by making a vibrant butterfly feeder.

YOU WILL NEED

★

Paper cup

Sharp pencil, scissors and string

Kitchen sponge

Coloured paper and glue

Apple juice

Field guide

Using the pencil, make two holes on opposite sides of the paper cup. The holes should be just below the rim of the cup. Cut a piece of string about 40cm (15½in) long. Poke the ends through the holes in the cup. Tie a knot at each end so the string makes a handle.

Using the pencil, make a hole in the centre of the bottom of the cup. Use the pencil to widen the hole. The hole should be a bit bigger than the width of the pencil. Cut a piece of sponge that is at least twice as big as the hole. Now push the sponge into the hole so half of it is sticking out.

It's time to decorate the cup. Butterflies are attracted to brightly coloured flowers, so cut out some paper flowers from the coloured paper. Make any design you like, then stick the flowers to the side of the cup.

Half-fill the cup with apple juice and hang it somewhere sunny in the garden, then watch and wait. Observe the butterflies as they come to feed. Butterflies feed using a hollow tube called a proboscis, which acts like a straw. When the butterfly is not feeding, the proboscis is curled up like a deflated party blower. When the butterfly is eating, the proboscis is unfurled. The butterfly below is called a Painted Lady. It's well known throughout much of the world.

Make a list of the butterflies that come to feed, and use a field guide to help identify them. You can experiment by swapping the apple juice for other flavoured juices or for sugar water. (Sugar water is one part sugar and ten parts water.) Do certain butterflies prefer certain flavours?

MARK AND RECAPTURE SNAILS

Many gardeners dislike snails because they eat crops and flowers, but snails play a vital role in our gardens, where they consume rotting leaves and other decaying plant matter. See what they get up to by marking and recapturing them.

There are many different species of snail. Some live on land and some live in the water. This experiment focuses on land-living snails. This is an activity for spring, summer or autumn, because this is when snails are most active.

Choose an area to hunt for snails. Snails avoid being out in the open too much as this makes them vulnerable to drying out, and to predators that may spot them and gobble them up. Look in nooks, crannies and other sheltered places. Snails can often be found inside the rims of plant pots, on the shady sides of walls, and in the leaf litter on the ground.

Find as many snails as you can in your chosen area. Pick them up carefully using your forefinger and thumb, and transfer them into the box or tub. Take care not to leave

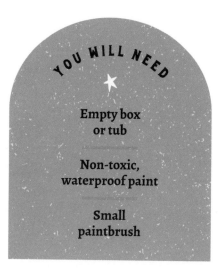

YOU WILL NEED

Empty box
or tub

Non-toxic,
waterproof paint

Small
paintbrush

Suppose you found ten snails on the first search. On the second search you found ten and two of these were marked. The total number of snails in the area is 10 × 10/2 = 50.

the box in bright sunshine as this could harm the snails. Make a note of the number of snails that you find.

Using the brush, place a tiny dot of paint onto the shell of each snail. Make sure to use non-toxic, waterproof paint that will wash off in the rain and leave the snail unharmed. Take care not to get paint on the snails' bodies, as they are very sensitive. Then release the snails back where you found them.

A few days later, go out and do another search. Make a note of how many new, non-marked snails you find, and how many paint-spotted individuals you manage to recapture.

You can work out how many snails are living in your area by multiplying the total number of snails from the first search by the total number of snails from the second search, and then dividing the answer by the number of marked snails from the second search.

BUILD A
DEAD HEDGE

Hedges that are made out of degrading plant material are called dead hedges. They're easy to make and great for wildlife. Build your own and find out what sorts of wildlife will move in.

Decide where you are going to make your dead hedge. Dead hedges are substantial structures that take up a bit of space, so you may want to check with an adult first. You can use them to create boundaries or to fence off key areas like ponds and wildflower meadows.

Normal hedges can take decades to grow, but dead hedges can be made in an afternoon. With a little maintenance, they can last for years.

Ask an adult to help you drive the posts into the ground with the mallet so they are standing upright. The posts should be about 4–8cm (1½–3in) in diameter. You can use tree branches or posts from a garden centre. It helps if the posts are sharpened at one end.

Arrange the first three posts so they form a row. Each post should be separated by a gap of about 50cm (20in). Tie a piece of garden string to one of the posts and then wind it back and forth between the posts so that it gives the boundary of the hedge some structure.

Make an identical second row of posts. There should be a 50cm (20in) gap between the two rows.

If you have any cuttings from stringy climbers like ivy or bendy trees like willow, you can weave them in and out of the posts to reinforce the string.

✳ Fill the gap between the two rows of posts with sticks, hedge cuttings and dead wood. Anything woody that takes a while to rot will do. Pile the items on top of one another until they reach the top of the posts. Press it down gently to compact it. Top up if necessary.

✳ Don't add green waste like grass clippings or leaf mulch, as this will rot too quickly and turn your dead hedge into a compost heap!

YOU WILL NEED

★

Six posts or stout sticks measuring about 1m (3ft) tall

Mallet

Garden string

Twigs, branches and other woody cuttings

✳ Sit back and watch the wildlife move in. Dead hedges provide homes for birds and small mammals, not to mention invertebrates like beetles and bees. Keep a record of what comes to visit, and compare what you find with the wildlife in and around a normal green hedge. Is there more or less wildlife in your dead hedge?

MAKE A
SOUND MAP

Sound maps are simply maps of the sounds that surround us. There are lots of interesting sounds in the garden. Take time to hear and record them by making your own sound map.

YOU WILL NEED
★

Ears

Notebook
and pen

★ We rarely take the time to stand still and listen to the noises that surround us, but it's an experience that can be deeply rewarding.

★ Head into the garden, find a spot and stand still. What can you hear? Sometimes it helps to close your eyes so you can concentrate on sounds rather than sights. At first, you'll notice things that are

familiar. It might be birdsong, the barking of a dog or the thrum of a neighbouring lawn mower.

★ Be still and silent. Now listen more deeply . . . what else can you hear? When you really stop to listen, you can hear all sorts of sounds. You may hear the rustling of wind in the trees, the buzzing of bees or the whining of tiny flies as they zoom past you. Every landscape has its own unique soundscape.

★ Write a list of all the sounds that you hear in 10 minutes. Now draw your map. Draw a picture of yourself in the centre of the map then position all the other sounds around you.

Maps show us where things are, and give us an idea of the distance between different objects. Try to make your map do the same. If the car was further away than the dog, for example, draw it further out on the map. If the dog was louder than the car, you may wish to make the dog bigger than the car.

Go back into the garden later in the day and repeat the process. How have the sounds changed? Are there any new noises? Maybe next time ask a friend to join you, then you can compare the sound maps that you both make. Different people often tune in to different sounds in their environment, so their map may be quite different to yours.

Make a sound map when you go somewhere different, like the seaside or the zoo. Compare the sounds from home with these new, exotic noises.

MAKE A HIBERNACULUM

A hibernaculum is a shelter that is used by animals to help them survive the cold. See if you can attract amphibians to your garden by building them a place where they can spend the winter.

YOU WILL NEED

★

Spade

Logs and branches

Bricks and rocks

Two or three drainpipe offcuts

Wildflower seeds

★ Find a spot for your hibernaculum. It's best to build it tucked out of the way, in a corner of the garden. You're about to create a very big hole, so make sure you're not about to uproot any important plants. Check with an adult to make sure the location is a suitable one.

★ Dig a hole that is about 150cm (60in) wide and 50cm (20in) deep. Pile up the earth you remove on the side of the hole. Fill the hole with logs, branches, bricks and rocks. They can be piled in messily but the idea is to leave lots of space between these items so there are cavities where the animals can hide.

★ Now for the drainpipe offcuts. If offcuts are difficult to come by, you can ask a local tradesman or DIY store if they have some spare. The offcuts should be roughly 30–50cm (12–20in) long. The drainpipes are going to be tunnels that connect the cold outside world with the warm, cosy hiding place.

✴ Push the drainpipes into the hole so they nestle between the rocks and logs. One end of the drainpipe should be poking out above ground so it is clearly visible. The drainpipes should be slanted at an angle so the residents can walk, hop or slither up and down the tunnels.

✴ Cover it all up with the soil that you removed, but make sure the entrances to the drainpipes are left open. Build up the soil into a mound. This will give the hibernaculum extra insulation. Sprinkle the mound with wildflower seeds and water them in.

DID YOU KNOW?
Lots of animals hibernate. It's a way to save energy in the cold. Bears build their own hibernacula inside caves, hillsides and gnarled old tree roots.

✴ Your hibernaculum is now good to go. These wintery hiding places attract small animals, like toads, lizards, snakes and insects. Monitor the hibernaculum and keep a record of what goes in and what comes out. But try not to disturb the creatures. List and draw the different species in your science journal.

WATER-BEAR HUNT

Water bears or tardigrades are tough, tiny creatures that can live just about anywhere, from the deep sea to mountaintops, from the tropics to Antarctica. They're enchanting to look at, so go on a water-bear hunt and see what you can find.

Go out and look for moss and lichen. Moss is often green and velvety. It tends to grow in clumps in damp and shady places. Lichens are often a green or blue-grey colour. They tend to be crusty and can be found growing on exposed surfaces. You may find lichen on stones, tree trunks, paving slabs or the sides of buildings. Scrape lots of moss and lichen into your clean plastic tub and bring the container home.

Water bears live in moss and lichen, but if it's too dry, the tiny creatures dry out and enter a state of suspended animation called cryptobiosis. Water reanimates them. Fill the container with rainwater and leave it overnight. If you don't have rainwater, use bottled spring water. Tap water contains chemicals that can harm the water bears.

The next day, scoop up the moss and lichen and squeeze it so all the water goes back into the plastic tub. Then pour a little of the water into a clean bowl or tray.

Water bears are so tiny that you'll need a magnifying device to see them. A microscope is ideal, but many smartphones now have a built-in magnifying function. Alternatively, you can buy a clip-on microscope that fits over the lens of a smartphone.

There will probably be lots of living things swimming about, so you need to know what you're looking for. Water bears have wrinkly bodies, scrunched up heads and four pairs of legs. They look like little bears but some people call them moss piglets because they look a bit pig-like too.

When you spot one, increase the magnification and take a photo for your journal. How many water bears can you see? Do samples from different places contain more or fewer water bears? Remember to set your water bears free when you are done.

YOU WILL NEED

Lichen and moss

Penknife

Plastic tub

Rainwater

Bowl or tray

Magnifying device

MAKE A
BIRD FEEDER

Food shortages can occur at any time of year, so give our feathered friends a helping hand by hanging up some homemade bird feeders. Test different designs to see which is more popular.

Different birds like different foods, so some bird feeders may be more popular than others. We're going to make two different types of feeder and then test them in the garden.

Which of your bird feeders is more popular? Do certain types of bird prefer one to the other? What times of day do the birds visit? Keep a note of your observations in your science journal.

For the first feeder, add the dry ingredients into a bowl. Garden birds will happily eat birdseed, but they'll also eat human food, such as bacon rind, raisins, breadcrumbs and grated cheese. Mix the ingredients together.

Soften the solid cooking fat by leaving it on a windowsill or a radiator. Add the cooking fat into the bowl and use a wooden spoon to mush all of the ingredients together. The cooking fat will bind the ingredients together.

Take a long piece of string and tie one end around the handle of the mug. Fill up the mug with the bird food mixture and push the garden twig into the hole, so it is half in,

FEEDER 1

Dry ingredients
such as birdseed,
grated cheese and
breadcrumbs

Hard cooking fat
such as lard

Wooden spoon,
string and twig

Bowl and old mug

FEEDER 2

Apple and
sunflower seeds

Two sticks about
15cm (6in) long

String and
scissors

half out. Now put the mug in the fridge so the fat becomes hard and sets around the twig.

★ Whilst it is setting, prepare the second bird feeder. Ask an adult to core an apple. (This means cutting a hole through the middle of the apple so the core can be removed.) Take a handful of sunflower seeds and push them into the fleshy part of the apple so the seeds are half sticking out.

★ Take two short sticks and cross them so they form an 'X' shape. Take a long piece of string and tie the crossed-over sticks together. Thread the long end of the string up through the apple core. The sticks make perches for the birds to stand on whilst they are eating the apple and the seeds.

★ Hang both feeders in the garden and wait for the birds to appear.

MAKE AN UNDERWATER VIEWER

Check out the underwater wildlife in a nearby pond or stream. Make an underwater viewing device called a bathyscope and record the aquatic life forms that live near you.

Cut the top and bottom off your plastic bottle to make a long hollow tube. You may need to ask an adult to help with this. Use the sandpaper to file down the freshly cut surfaces so there are no sharp edges.

Stretch the clear plastic over one end of the bathyscope. It's good to recycle, so you could use an old, clear plastic bag, or you could use the clear plastic wrapping that is sometimes used to protect fresh fruit and vegetables. Secure the plastic in place using an elastic band. Make sure it's stretched tight so you can see through it clearly.

The bathyscope needs to be watertight, so once the plastic is in place, wrap duct tape around

YOU WILL NEED
★

Large plastic bottle

Scissors

Sandpaper

Clear plastic bag

Rubber band

Duct tape

the outside of the bottle so the plastic becomes stuck to the side. This should prevent any water from leaking into the bathyscope when you use it.

Find a local pond or stream. It's time to test the bathyscope out. Pond dipping is all well and good, but a bathyscope enables you to see underwater animals and plants in their natural environment. Kneel down near the edge of the pond or stream and place the plastic-covered end in the water. Don't lean over too far or you could fall in. Now, peer through the other end. What do you see?

Compare different types of habitats. The critters that live in ponds may be slightly different to the ones that live in moving water, such as streams and rivers. If you live close to the sea, you could try looking in rock pools. Extra points if you spot any fast-moving fish! Draw what you see and record your findings in your science journal. What is the most exciting animal that you spotted?

If you're feeling really adventurous, go large! Make a bathyscope from a bucket or a refuse bin, then place it in the water and see what you can find.

THE GREAT SNAIL RACE

Blink and you won't miss it! Find out what surfaces suit snails the best by organising a snail race.

YOU WILL NEED

Five garden snails

Cardboard

Plank of wood

Soil

Tray

First, find some garden snails. Snails like cool, damp, shady environments that are close to food sources. If your garden has a vegetable patch, there are likely to be snails hiding away in the foliage. Try looking under and around plant pots, or around climbing plants that are growing up walls. Collect five snails. Handle them carefully and wash your hands once the experiment is done.

Prepare the racetracks. There will be three circular tracks made of wood, cardboard and soil. Mark out the first two tracks: one on a large piece of wood, and one on a large piece of card. To make the soil racetrack, lay out a circle of soil in a tray. Make sure the circles are all the same size.

Can you feel the excitement mounting? Place the snails in the centre of the first wooden racetrack. Time how long it takes each individual to reach the edge of the track. Make a note of these times. Calculate the average time by adding up all of the individual times and dividing them by five.

Now test the snails on the second track made of cardboard. Place the same snails in the centre and time how long it takes each individual to reach the edge. Calculate the average. Repeat the experiment one last time using the third track, which is made of soil. Calculate the average.

Measure the distance from the starting place to the edge of the track. Now calculate the average speed on each track: speed equals distance divided by time. Ask an adult to help you convert your calculations into a measurement that is in metres (or feet) per second. Which surface were they speediest on?

See if you can design a racetrack that makes the snails even faster. Would the racetrack be bumpy or smooth, wet or dry? What's the fastest speed your snails can achieve? Record the results in your journal.

WONDERFUL WILDLIFE

QUIZ

Once you've tried a few of the experiments in this section, you'll be surprised at how quickly your understanding of the natural world can grow. Test your new-found knowledge with this little quiz.

1. Did you find an activity that you really enjoyed? Name the single, best experiment in this section of the book.

2. Moths can be unexpectedly vibrant and beautiful. Explain two different ways to attract moths to your garden.

3. Can you describe three different ways to encourage wildlife into your garden?

4. In winter, resources are scarce so some animals snooze the cold months away. Can you name four different animals that hibernate?

5. Bathe in the beauty of birdsong. Can you recognise five different bird songs?

6. They're not creepy, but they are crawly. Can you name a garden-dwelling animal that has six legs?

7. Garden birds benefit from additional food. Can you list seven foods that garden birds like to eat?

8. They play a vital part in the garden ecosystem. Can you name a garden-dwelling animal that has eight legs?

9. Ponds are havens for life. Can you draw nine different water-living animals that can be found in ponds?

10. They're a joy to watch and welcome into our gardens. Can you recognise ten different garden birds?

11. Our gardens are full of life. Can you draw eleven different land-living animals that live in your garden?

12. The garden is full of noise. Can you describe twelve different garden sounds you hear every day?

Do you know . . .

★ How to devise your own experiment and write it up? Scientists always write up their experiments.

★ Why birds sing? It's an important part of their life.

★ How to build a bug hotel? Welcoming bugs into your garden can be a rewarding experience.

★ Where woodlice like to live? They're not difficult to find. Pick up a plant pot and look underneath.

★ How hoverfly larvae breathe underwater? Think of them if you ever go snorkelling.

★ Which part of a butterfly's body is used to taste things? Aren't insects amazing!

★ How to collect insects in an umbrella? Just remember to set them free before you use the umbrella on a rainy day.

★ What a mouse footprint looks like? They're very distinctive.

★ Where to look for water bears? They live just about everywhere but are so small you've probably never noticed them.

★ How to prevent the water in a birdbath from freezing? When the cold comes, the birds will thank you for it.

★ How toads catch their food? Can you think of any other animals that catch their food the same way?

SOIL
SCIENCE

Soil is really remarkable. The next time
you're walking in your garden or local park,
stop for a moment and think about the soil
that's under your feet. We walk all over it every
day and hardly give it a moment's thought.
Some people might assume it's dull and boring,
but soil is brimming with life and life-giving
properties. It's time we learned to appreciate
soil and all the things it does for us.

SOIL SCIENCE

Soil is a gloriously grubby mixture of organic and inorganic matter. Organic matter is anything that comes from living things. Fallen leaves, grass cuttings and animal droppings are all examples of organic matter. Inorganic matter is made up of non-living substances. Pebbles and rocks are inorganic, but soil also contains tiny inorganic particles of things like sand, silt and clay.

Soil is amazing for many reasons. It is a life-support machine. It provides plants with the water and nutrients that they need to survive and grow. We need soil to grow the crops that feed us and that feed the livestock we eat.

Soil is a home. It's teeming with living things, such as bacteria, fungi, like the toadstool Fly Agaric (below), and worms. These

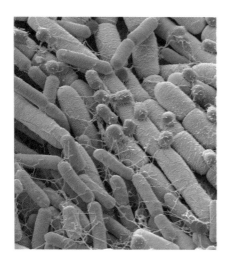

Soil is so much more than dirt. In this chapter, you'll be learning more about the soil in your neighbourhood. You'll be testing it to see how acid or alkaline it is, how much water it retains and how much air it holds. You'll be learning about its makeup, and the vital role that soil plays in helping living things to decompose. You'll be making compost, so you can nourish the plants that are growing nearby, and learning about the minibeasts that make soil their home. Most of all, you'll be learning how to appreciate this most grubby and under-appreciated marvel – so next time an adult moans about the dirt on your clothes, you can tell them how important it is!

underground marvels work hard to improve the quality of the soil. Bacteria (above), for example, convert nitrogen in the air into soil-based forms of nitrogen that plants can use for growth. Fungi help to break down fallen leaves and dead animals, releasing nutrients into the soil. Earthworms (below) dig tunnels that break up the soil and improve drainage, making it easier for plants to grow.

Soil is a filter. It doesn't only store water. The tiny particles in soil also help to cleanse water of harmful chemicals and pollutants. When plants grow in soil, their roots form tangled networks that help to stabilise the soil and bind it together. This helps to prevent erosion and flooding.

COMPOST JARS

If living things didn't decompose after they died, the world would be chock-full of waste. Fortunately, microorganisms are on hand to break down organic material. Set up some see-through compost jars and time how long it takes for different materials to degrade.

★ Remove the lids from the jars and make some holes in them by banging the nail into the lid – remove the nail with the claw of the hammer. You might need an adult to help with this task. Make sure you keep your thumb out of the way when banging in the nail!

★ Half-fill the jars with soil from the garden. If the soil is dry, sprinkle it with water, but don't add too much. The soil should not become waterlogged.

★ Add the fillings. Add the banana skin to one jar, and a crumpled-up piece of newspaper to another. To the third jar, add a scrunched-up biodegradable plastic bag. Many dog poo bags are biodegradable, so these are perfect.

Top up the jars with soil, but make sure the fillings are still visible. If you have a mercury thermometer, gently press it into the soil and record the temperature in the centre of each jar. Make a note of this. Now screw on the lids and put the jars somewhere warm, like a windowsill.

It takes a while for organic material to decompose, so be prepared to wait. Check the jars every week. What differences do you notice? Are the fillings beginning to break down? Unscrew the lid of each jar and take further temperature readings. Note these down. When living things decompose, they release heat, so you should notice an increase in temperature.

Let the experiment run for two to three months, then empty the jars and see what has happened. Which of the three different fillings has decomposed? Which item degraded first and which took the longest? If an item has yet to decay, put it back in the jar and keep the experiment running. Time how long it takes.

MAKE IT GROW FASTER

Plants need more than just water and sunlight to grow. They also need nutrients like nitrogen. Fertilisers contain nitrogen. See how well they work by growing some plants with and without fertiliser.

YOU WILL NEED

Ten medium
plant pots

Potting soil, topsoil

Packet of
sunflower seeds

Water

Houseplant
fertiliser

Two large plastic
bottles

Add an equal amount of potting soil mixed with some topsoil to each of the plant pots. Fill the pots to the top then press the soil down with your fingers. Topsoil is just the top layer of soil in the ground.

Choose ten equally sized sunflower seeds from the packet. Add one seed to each pot. Place each seed gently on top of the soil, then cover it up with a thin layer of potting soil. Moisten the soil in each pot by adding an equal amount of water.

Label five of the pots with 'fertiliser' and five of the pots with 'water'. Place all of the pots on a sunny windowsill and leave them to grow.

Label one of the bottles with 'fertiliser' and the other with 'water'. Fill the 'water' bottle with water, then prepare the fertiliser. Many common household fertilisers come as concentrated powders or liquids that need to be diluted with water. Carefully following the instructions on the packet, prepare enough fertiliser to fill the 'fertiliser' bottle.

When the soil starts to dry out, the plants need watering. Always add an equal amount of liquid to each seedling. Always water the 'fertiliser' plants with fertiliser, and the 'water' plants with water. Depending on the temperature, the plants may need watering two to three times per week. Make up more fertiliser as you need it.

Once a week, measure the plants. Make a note of how tall they are and how many leaves they have sprouted. Do you notice anything else? Sunflowers can really shoot up, so as they grow, the plants may need supporting with sticks. If they get really big, they may need moving into a larger pot. If you do this, re-pot all of the plants at the same time.

Although the air is full of nitrogen, plants can't use it directly. Instead, they rely on soil-dwelling microbes that convert atmospheric nitrogen into other, more plant-friendly forms.

After a few months, analyse the data. Which plants are the tallest? Is there a difference between 'fertiliser' and 'water' plants? Plot a graph showing how each plant has grown over time.

TEST YOUR SOIL'S pH

pH is a measure of how acidic or alkaline something is. Some plants like to grow in soil that is more acidic, whilst others like to grow in earth that is more alkaline. Find out what the soil in your garden is like by using this simple test.

YOU WILL NEED

Two shallow dishes or saucers

Soil

Kitchen vinegar and distilled water

Baking powder

Fill the shallow dishes with soil from the garden. The soil should be fairly dry. If it's too wet, put the saucers on a windowsill and let the soil dry out before you continue.

Sprinkle about five tablespoons of vinegar onto the soil in the first dish and watch what happens next. If the soil fizzes and bubbles you are likely to have alkaline soil.

Sprinkle a tablespoonful of baking powder over the second saucer of soil, then wet the mixture by pouring a little distilled water over it. If it fizzes or bubbles, the soil in your garden is very acidic.

Grab a handful of soil and rub your hands with it. This will get rid of any products, such as soap or moisturiser that are already on your skin and could affect the experiment.

If nothing happens when you add vinegar or baking powder, then the soil in your garden is likely to have a neutral pH.

If you saw bubbles in this experiment, they were caused by a chemical reaction. When acidic and alkaline things meet, water and carbon dioxide gas are formed. Bubbles of carbon dioxide rise to the top of the mixture – just like they would in a fizzy drink – and cause the liquid to fizz.

DID YOU KNOW?
pH is measured on a scale of 0 to 14. A pH of 7 is neutral. A pH of less than 7 is acidic, and a pH of more than 7 is alkaline. Most plants like a pH somewhere between 6 and 7.

Look up which plants prefer the soil type that you have in your garden. Could this explain why some plants grow better than others?

If you want to find out the pH of your soil more accurately, try to borrow some pH paper from school. Dip the paper into some watery soil. Wait for the paper to change colour then compare the result to the colour chart that comes with the strips. This will give you a numerical value for the soil pH. You could also try making an indicator dye from red cabbage (see pages 152–53).

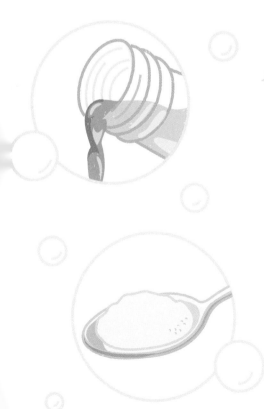

SOIL TEXTURE EXPERIMENT

Some gardens have light, sandy soil. Others have heavy, clay soil. There are many different types of soil. Find out which type of soil is in your garden using this simple texture test.

Three-quarters fill the glass jar with soil from the garden. Make sure there are no pebbles or large stones in the soil. If there are any big clumps of soil, break them apart with your fingers first and crumble the soil into the jar.

Add a tablespoon of laundry detergent and a tablespoon of salt to the soil. Top up the jar with water. Stir the mixture using the spoon then screw the lid on tightly. The ingredients need to be really well mixed, so shake the jar for 5 minutes.

Put the jar on a windowsill and leave it for a few days. Don't pick it up or disturb the jar during this time. After a couple of days, the soil will settle into different layers.

Soil is made from different types of particle. Sand particles are the heaviest, so they will sink to the bottom. Clay particles are the lightest, so they will settle on the top. Silt is a grainy material. Silt particles are medium-sized, so if there is silt in your soil, it will form a layer in the middle, between the sand and the clay.

You can estimate how much of each different type of particle are in your soil by measuring the thickness of the different layers. If the sand layer at the bottom is really thick, for example, then you have sandy soil.

Sandy soils are easy to dig but they dry out easily and are low in nutrients. This means they need regular watering and topping up with fertilisers. Clay soils are heavy and can be difficult to dig. They are rich in nutrients and retain water well, but can become waterlogged making it harder for plants to grow. Silt soils are somewhere in the middle.

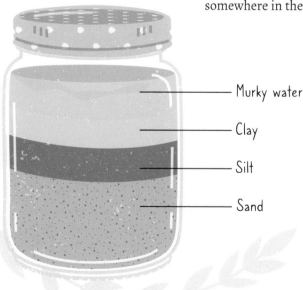

Murky water

Clay

Silt

Sand

MAKE A LEAF COMPOST BIN

Compost is made of organic material that has decomposed. It contains lots of nutrients that help plants to grow. Make some leaf compost in a simple compost bin and give your plants a treat.

★ This is an activity for autumn when there are lots of fallen leaves around. Decide where you want your compost bin to go. It takes a year or more to make leaf compost, so it is best to choose a spot that's out of the way and won't be needed for anything else.

★ Mark out the compost bin. You can make it any size you like, but it doesn't have to be huge. A square that is 1m × 1m (3ft × 3ft) works well.

★ The bamboo canes are going to form the corners of the square. The canes should be about 1m (3ft) tall. Carefully push the canes into the ground so they stand upright without support.

You may need someone to help you with this next step. Unroll the netting and wrap it around the four bamboo canes. If you are using chicken wire, wear gloves for this as it can be sharp. The netting should go all the way round the square once, with a little extra to form an overlap.

Cut some small pieces of garden wire and use them to tie the netting to the bamboo canes. Use at least two ties per cane: one at the top and one at the bottom. Use some extra pieces of wire to tie the two ends of the netting together where they overlap. Trim any excess using scissors or wire cutters. Your leaf compost bin is ready to go!

Leaves don't turn to compost on their own. The mixture is broken down by tiny organisms, like bacteria and fungi.

Collect lots of leaves and pile them up in the compost bin. Use leaves that have already fallen from deciduous trees. Deciduous leaves degrade more quickly than leaves from evergreen trees, so it helps to speed up the composting process.

If the leaves start to dry out, water the compost bin. In a year or two, the leaves will rot away to form a rich, nutritious compost.

SOIL EROSION EXPERIMENT

When soil is washed away, any nutrients or chemicals inside the soil get washed away too. This is a big problem because it can pollute rivers and streams, and harm wildlife. Find out how to stabilise soil and prevent this soil erosion.

YOU WILL NEED

Three foil food trays

Three white dinner plates

Soil and grass seed

Pencil and scissors

Leaves and small rocks

Three thick books

Water and watering can

Use a pencil to poke ten drainage holes in the bottom of the three food trays. The holes should be about the same width as a pencil.

Prepare the first food tray. Label it 'Grass'. Fill it with soil and generously sprinkle the grass seeds on top. Lightly water the seeds so the soil becomes damp. Place the tray on one of the plates and put it on a windowsill. Leave it for a few weeks, and remember to water it regularly. When the grass has grown nice and thick, you can continue with the next stage.

Fill the second and third food trays with soil. Lightly water the soil, so it is roughly as damp as the soil in the 'Grass' tray. Label the second tray 'Leaves and stones', then add a layer of leaves and small stones on top of the soil. Label the third tray 'Soil only'. The third tray is ready to go.

Use scissors to carefully cut off one of the small ends from each tray. This is now the front end. The trays should all now have three sides. Place each of the trays on a dinner plate.

Plant roots form a tangled mesh that helps to keep soil in place. Leaves and stones also help to prevent soil from being washed away.

The trays need to be at an angle, so prop a thick book underneath the back end of each tray. The front end should be pointing downwards towards the plate. This simulates a hill.

Now it's time to make it rain. Do this part of the experiment outside. Water the trays, one at a time, using a watering can. Hold the watering can up high so the water is sprinkled all over the tray. Count to ten whilst you water each tray, then stop.

Look at the water that collects in each of the plates. How much soil is there in each of the plates? Did the grass or the leaves and stones help to prevent erosion?

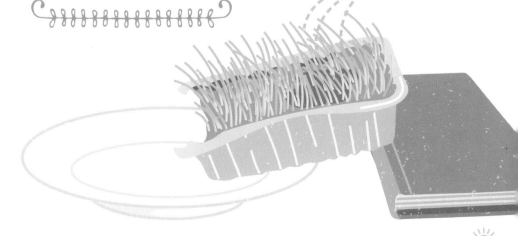

SOIL FILTRATION EXPERIMENT

Soil acts as a natural filter. It can trap certain pollutants and chemicals, which helps to purify water. 'Pollute' water with food colouring then clean it up with some natural soil filters.

YOU WILL NEED

Three large plastic bottles

Three glass jars

Stones and scissors

Topsoil and sand

Moss or green leaves

Jug of water and cup

Red and blue food colouring

Cut the bottom off the plastic bottles. Turn the bottles upside down and rest them on the open glass jars. Put a tightly packed layer of stones at the bottom of each bottle. The stones need to be bigger than the mouth of the bottle to stop them from falling through.

To the first bottle, add a thick layer of sand (c. 10cm/4in). To the second bottle, add a thick layer of topsoil (c. 10cm/4in). Topsoil is the top layer of soil that you find in the garden. To the third bottle, add a thick layer of topsoil followed by an additional layer of moss or green leaves. You can be creative with this last layer. Add in anything from the garden that you think will help to filter the water.

Mix up your food colouring. Add red and blue food colouring to a jug of water to make a deep purple colour. This is your pretend pollutant. Pour an equal volume of the pollutant into each of the bottles and watch what happens.

The liquid will trickle through the bottle and some will collect in the jar underneath. This is called the filtrate. If no liquid is coming out, add another cupful of the pollutant to each of the jars.

Don't be disappointed if the filtrate is cloudy or dirty. This often happens at the start of the experiment. Pour the dirty water away and keep pouring more pollutant into the bottles.

Look at the colour of the filtrate in each jar. Which is the most purple? This water still contains 'pollutants'. It has not been well filtered. Which is the clearest? This is water that has been well filtered.

Soil that is rich in silt or clay acts as a good natural filter. Large particles become trapped in the thick heavy soil, whilst water molecules can eventually pass through.

'Pollutant'

Filtrate

MINI WORMERY

Worms are the unsung heroes of the underground. They break down plant matter, churn up the soil and enrich the earth with their droppings. Find out about their vital recycling role by making them a temporary home.

YOU WILL NEED

Plant pot

Paints and a brush

Plastic bottle

Scissors and sticky tape

Soil and sand

Grass clippings and a few pebbles (optional)

Two or three worms

Newspaper

★ Brighten up your plant pot by giving it a lick of paint! You could even paint a sign saying, 'WORMS LIVE HERE'. Leave it to dry.

★ Using the scissors, cut the top and bottom off the plastic bottle to create a see-through plastic tube. This can be tricky so you may need adult help. Be careful! The edges of the tube might be sharp.

DID YOU KNOW?
The Giant Gippsland earthworm of Australia can grow to over 2m (6ft) long.

✳ Place the tube in the plant pot so it stands upright. Fill around the outside of the tube with soil to make it more stable. Now fill the inside of the tube with alternating layers of sand and soil. Earthworms like to live in damp earth, so sprinkle each layer with a bit of water. The soil layers should be about the width of your thumb and the sand layers should be a little thinner.

✳ Leave some space at the top of the tube to add in the grass cuttings. Earthworms feed on living matter, so the grass will provide them with food.

✳ With the grass in place, go outside and find some worms. They'll be hiding in the soil. If you can't find them, try soaking the ground with a hose for 10 minutes. This will help to bring any earthworms up to the surface. These are living creatures, so handle them with care.

✳ Add two or three earthworms to the top of your wormery, and watch as they bury down into the soil. Worms live in the dark, so wrap the newspaper around the tube and fasten it with a piece of tape. This will make it dark and encourage the worms to visit the edges of the tube where you can see them when you remove the paper cover.

✳ Put the wormery in a cool, dark place and check it each day. Watch how grass disappears and the layers get mixed up. Record how long it takes for the grass to disappear. Make a note in your science journal. After a few days, return the worms to a safe place in the garden.

HOW MUCH AIR IS IN YOUR SOIL?

It may just look like mud, but soil contains a lot of air. This includes oxygen, which helps plants and animals to breathe, and nitrogen which helps to nourish plants. Find out the air content of different soil samples using this simple experiment.

Collect three different soil samples. You will need a handful of each. Choose samples from different locations. Perhaps one from the garden, one from a hedgerow, and one from a riverbank. Try to choose samples that look and feel different.

YOU WILL NEED

★

Three different soils

Water and water sprayer

Three glass jars or jugs

Smartphone

If the samples are dry, moisten them using water from the sprayer. Mould each sample into a ball. The balls should all be roughly the same size and be able to fit inside the glass jars.

Fill the glass jars three-quarters full with water. Drop the first soil sample into the first jar and film what happens next. What do you see? Tiny air bubbles will be released from the soil sample into the water. They float up to the surface and then disappear.

Up to 50 per cent of soil is made up of gases, such as oxygen, carbon dioxide and nitrogen. If the soil is waterlogged or compacted, there is less space for air and this can make life difficult for soil-dwelling organisms.

It's hard to count the number of bubbles that are released in real time, which is where your video recording comes in. Play back the video – at half speed if you can – and count how many bubbles are released from the sample.

Now repeat the same process with the second and third samples. Make a table in your journal, detailing the number of bubbles released from each sample. Which sample had the most air? Which sample had the least air? What do you think this means for the animals and plants that live in these different soils?

Repeat the experiment using soil from the same sites, but this time dig down. Compare soil from the surface with soil that is around 20cm (8in) down. Keep digging. Collect a third sample that is as far down as you can dig. What do you notice? The soil from the surface should have much more air than the soil from lower down.

HOW MUCH WATER CAN YOUR SOIL HOLD?

It's important for soil to be able to retain water, because plants need water to grow. Different soils hold different amounts of water. Try this experiment to work out how much water the soil from your garden can hold.

YOU WILL NEED

Soil, sand and clay

Funnel

Three coffee filters

Glass jar

Measuring jug

Kitchen scales

Collect a big handful of soil. This can come from the ground in your garden, or from a plant pot where you grow something. Using the kitchen scales, weigh out 50g (1.8oz) of your soil.

Place the funnel into the glass jar and place a coffee filter inside the funnel. Make sure the coffee filter is open. Add the soil to the filter, just as you would add coffee for a hot drink.

Measure out 50ml (1.8fl oz)of water in the measuring jug. Slowly pour the water over the soil. Wait for 5 minutes. What happens? Some of the water will pass through the soil and drip through the funnel into the jar underneath. Pour the water into the empty measuring jug. How much did you manage to collect?

Now repeat the experiment with a fresh soil sample, but this time find out what happens when you add some sand to the soil. Sand is part of the natural makeup of soil but some soils are sandier than others. Did you collect more or less water this time?

Repeat the experiment one last time, with another fresh soil sample. This time crumble some dried clay into the soil. Clay is also found in many soils. How much water did you collect during this final part of the experiment?

Make a note of the results in your journal. Why do you think the experiments gave different results?

Optimise the amount of water your garden soil holds. Add sand to improve drainage. Add compost or clay to improve water retention.

Sand particles are larger than clay particles, so there are more spaces or 'pores' for the water to filter through. So, if you want to improve the drainage in your garden, add some sand. Clay particles are smaller than sand particles. They sit snugly next to one another, so there aren't many pores at all. This means that clay soils retain more water than sandy soils. This can be handy if you live somewhere hot where it doesn't rain much.

FANTASTIC FACTS

It's gloriously grubby and downright dirty, but soil is a haven for life and a crucial part of many different ecosystems. It might seem brown and boring, but soil is also packed full of interesting facts. Here are a few that will impress any soil sceptics that you might know.

★ One-quarter of all the world's known species live in soil. That's millions of different species, but only 1 per cent of microscopic soil-dwelling species have been identified. If you look carefully, you might even discover a new species!

★ One teaspoon of garden soil contains thousands of different species of living things, but most of them are so small, they are invisible to the naked eye. This includes microscopic creatures like bacteria and some fungi.

★ Soil takes many hundreds of years to form. Soil is formed when rocks get broken down into tiny microscopic pieces. This is called weathering. Rocks are responsible for the minerals that are found inside soil.

★ Healthy soils aren't always brown. Depending on the minerals and organic matter present, they can be red, yellow, black, white, green or grey. Brown soil contains lots of organic matter, whilst greenish soil contains a mineral called glauconite.

★ British scientist Charles Darwin loved worms. He called them 'nature's ploughs' because of their ability to mix soil and organic matter, and he tested their ability to hear by playing them his bassoon.

★ Worms are amongst the most recognisable soil dwellers. There are more than 5,000 different species of worm. The Fried Egg Worm (above) from the Philippines looks like it has tiny fried eggs scattered along its body.

★ We all know that trees are important because they help to lock away atmospheric carbon dioxide, but did you know that soil stores more carbon than all the world's forests? When living things die and rot away, the carbon they contain is transferred to the soil.

★ Without soil, we'd be very hungry. Ninety-five per cent of the food we eat comes from the soil. You can add eggshells, tea bags and coffee grounds to your compost heap. They contain lots of molecules that help plants to grow.

★ When forests are cut down to make way for big industrial farms, the crops use up the nutrients and soil becomes less fertile. This puts soil in danger. Every minute around the world we lose the equivalent of thirty football pitches of soil. We need healthy soil to feed the world.

FASCINATING FLORA

〰〰〰〰〰〰〰〰〰〰〰〰〰〰〰

If you were to weigh all of the living
things on our planet, including animals,
plants, fungi, bacteria and viruses, you would
find that you need a very big pair of scales.
In addition, you would also find that plants
make up more than 80 per cent of the total
amount. We live on a planet covered in
plants. They are vital to our survival, so it's
time we learned to love them.

〰〰〰〰〰〰〰〰〰〰〰〰〰〰〰

FASCINATING FLORA

Plants are phenomenally successful. They grow just about everywhere: in the heat of the desert like the Beavertail cactus (opposite), in the icy wastelands of the Arctic like Cotton-grass (opposite below), and in the inhospitable cracks and crevices of buildings and streets.

The smallest plants are made of a single cell, whilst the tallest plants – evergreen redwood trees – tower more than 100m (330ft) above

the ground (see below). Plants give us glorious displays of colour and inviting places to explore. They provide us with food, medicines and building materials, but more than that, they give us the very oxygen that we breathe.

Powered by sunshine, plants absorb carbon dioxide from the air, combine it with water, and convert it into sugars and oxygen. The sugars are used by the plants to

you work out the age and height of your favourite tree, and understand why it is that leaves change colour in the autumn. You'll be growing plants from food scraps and store-cupboard seeds, and making leaves disintegrate so you can see their skeletons. You'll be creating vegetable animals, making flowers change colour and growing your name in cress. One minute you'll be lovingly growing seedlings in a greenhouse, and the next you'll be smashing up plants with a hammer. It's time to enjoy the wonderful world of plants!

help them grow, whilst the oxygen is released into the atmosphere. This process is called photosynthesis and it's the reason some people call trees the 'lungs of the earth'. They help the planet to breathe.

As humans pump carbon dioxide into the atmosphere and rainforests are felled to make way for food crops, we need trees more than ever before. They help to mop up carbon dioxide, and so can help us to control climate change.

It's time we appreciated how important plants are. In this section, you'll explore how plants grow, and the different things that they need to keep them strong and healthy. There are experiments to help

PHOTOTROPISM BOX

Plants need light to help them grow, so they always grow towards it. This is called phototropism. Perform an experiment to demonstrate phototropism using a cardboard box, a potato and some sunshine.

YOU WILL NEED

Shoebox with lid

Scissors and sticky tape

Cardboard

One potato (with eyes)

Small plant pot

Soil and water

Knife

Cardboard

Stand the shoebox on its smallest side so it stands upright, long and tall. Using scissors, make a hole in the middle of the 'roof' of the shoebox. The hole should be about 3cm × 3cm (1in × 1in).

Make two cardboard shelves to fit inside the shoebox. Mark out the shelves on the cardboard by drawing around the base of the shoebox when it is standing upright. Cut them out. The shelves now need to be trimmed. Cut 4cm (1½in) off the end of each rectangle.

Fit the shelves inside the shoebox using sticky tape. The two shelves should split the box into three equal parts. The bottom shelf should be fixed to one wall of the box, and the top shelf should be fixed to the opposite wall. The shelves will prevent the light from falling directly onto the potato plant and create obstacles that the shoot needs to grow around.

Prepare your plant. You need an old potato that has started to sprout eyes. The eyes are the beginnings of new shoots that are starting to grow. Fill the plant pot with soil. If the soil is dry, water it a little, but take care the soil doesn't become waterlogged. Cut the potato in half and press the freshly cut side down onto the soil.

Place the plant pot into the bottom of the shoebox. Close the shoebox and secure the lid by putting tape around it. Put the shoebox on a warm windowsill and leave it for a couple of weeks. Once a week, open the box up and check to see if the plant needs watering. Then seal it back up again.

DID YOU KNOW?
Photo means light.
Plants contain special
hormones that help
them to grow towards
the light.

After three weeks, you should see a green shoot poking out of the hole at the top of the box. The experiment is now complete. Draw a diagram to show how the plant grew. Did the shoot grow around the shelves to get to the light?

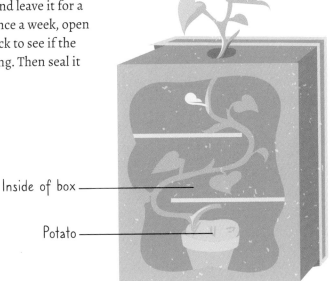

Inside of box ———

Potato ———

HAPA ZOME

Hapa Zome is the Japanese art of beating leaves and flowers with a hammer in order to make natural prints on fabric. Give it a go! It's easy and effective, and the results are beautiful.

YOU WILL NEED

Leaves and flowers

Plain cotton fabric

Breadboard

Hammer

Go in the garden and choose some leaves and flowers. They should be as varied as possible. Look for different shapes and sizes. Choose a variety of colours. White flowers won't make a mark on white fabric, so pick blooms with bright or dark-coloured petals. The leaves and flowers should be freshly picked.

Ones that are full of moisture work the best, so make sure you collect fresh, healthy specimens.

Prepare your fabric. Plain white fabric works but you could go for any light-coloured cloth. Thin cotton fabrics work well, so you could cut up an old pillowcase or bed sheet (but make sure you check with an adult first). Cut a piece of fabric that is the size of the image you want to make. Now cut a second identical piece.

Lay the first piece of fabric on a breadboard or other flat surface. Position the leaves and flowers on the fabric, arranging them into the design that you would like to see printed. Now lay the second piece of fabric over the top.

Here's where the fun starts. Gently tap the fabric with the hammer. If you don't have a hammer, or aren't allowed to use one, a rolling pin or smooth rock works just as well. Be gentle. Don't batter the fabric. Tap at it lightly. What do you see? The pattern of the plants should begin to appear.

Once you have flattened all of the plants, peel away the top layer of fabric. Remove the leaves and flowers. The dye from the plants will have transferred onto the two pieces of cotton. Hang them up to dry, then enjoy!

What will you do with your Hapa Zome prints? If you want to make bunting, you can cut them into triangles and thread them onto a piece of string. Alternatively, the prints make great wall hangings, and if you stick them onto cardboard, they make stunning greeting cards.

MAKE A
PLANT PRESS

You can keep a record of the plants that grow in your garden by pressing and drying them. Pressed flowers and plants are also really great for using in arts and crafts projects. It's easy to make a simple press out of recycled materials.

YOU WILL NEED

★

Newspaper
(small sheets are easier)

Corrugated cardboard

Two flat pieces of wood,
of equal size

Two belts, luggage straps
or bungee cords,
or string

Freshly picked
garden plants

Fold the newspaper sheets down the middle, where the fold normally is. These newspaper sheets will be your 'blotters', soaking up the moisture from the plants. Assemble them into sets of three, so that you can open and close each set together, like a mini newspaper.

Cut rectangles of cardboard so that they're the same size as your folded newspaper sheets. The tunnels in the corrugated cardboard will allow air to flow through your press.

Start by putting a sheet of cardboard on top of the wood base, then a set of three

newspaper sheets. Open up the sheets and place a plant in the centre, then close them so the plant has three sheets of paper on either side.

Add another piece of cardboard to the stack, and then another set of newspaper sheets, and another plant. Keep going until you've put all of your plants into newspaper in the stack.

Finish the stack with a last layer of cardboard, and then place the second piece of wood on top.

Now you need to put the straps around the press to hold it tightly closed. You can tie the press together with string, like a parcel, if you don't have straps.

Leave the plants in the press for 24 hours, and then you can check on them if you want to. You'll find that they take a few days to dry completely, and then you can reuse your press to flatten more plants – remember to use fresh newspaper.

Botanists press specimens of plants they find on their travels around the world, and these are kept in special libraries called herbaria. A herbarium can tell us a lot about where different plants grow.

FLOWER DISSECTION

Some flowers are simple, others are complex. These more complicated flowers contain rows and rows of petals, all tightly packed around a central core. Dissect a flower to create a work of art, and learn how the different parts of a flower fit together.

Get your hands on some fresh flowers. These can be cut flowers from the supermarket, or wildflowers from the garden. Choose a variety of different flowers, but be sure to include some with large bright petals.

DID YOU KNOW?
The world's biggest flower is the Rafflesia. It comes from the rainforest of Indonesia where it can grow up to 1m (39in) across. Imagine dissecting that!

Flowers have lots of different parts. The sepals are the small green leaves on the outside of a blossom. They help to protect the developing flower buds. Draw a stalk on your piece of paper then glue the sepals around the top of the stalk in a semi-circle.

Petals are actually modified leaves. Pull off the petals and stick them in a semi-circle around the sepals. If you have lots of petals, you'll need to make extra rows of semi-circles that radiate outwards.

Is there anything of the flower left? The inside contains the flower's reproductive parts. Most flowers have male parts called stamens and female parts called carpels. Stamens

Repeat the experiment using different types of flower. Do you notice a difference between plants that are insect-pollinated and plants that are wind-pollinated?

Insect-pollinated plants have brightly coloured petals, which help to attract pollinators like butterflies and bees. The petals of wind-pollinated plants are often dull green or brown because they don't need to attract insects.

The stamens of insect-pollinated plants are often stiff and firmly attached to the inside of the flower, so the insects can brush against them. The stamens of wind-pollinated plants often dangle down outside the flower, so they can release their pollen easily when there is a breeze.

are long filamentous structures that have blobs of pollen at the end. The carpel is the central structure that contains the ovary. Carefully pull off the stamens and carpel, and glue them onto the paper. This is the final, outer row.

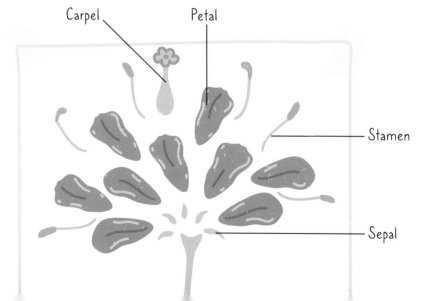

Carpel

Petal

Stamen

Sepal

MAKE A VEGETABLE ANIMAL

Let your imagination run wild with this test of creative thinking. Create a vegetable animal using only local fruit and vegetables that are in season.

These days, it's all too easy to buy seasonal food items, like raspberries and lettuces, all year round. Often the items are grown abroad and then transported vast distances to our supermarkets. This requires a lot of energy, making fruit and vegetables that are produced in this way less environmentally friendly than seasonal, locally grown produce.

Find out what fruits and vegetables are available locally. If you grow fruit and vegetables in your garden, ask a grown-up if you can use them for this project. If you don't, head to a farmer's market where local, seasonal products will be on sale. To keep costs down, ask stallholders if you can have produce that is past its best. They may give it to you for free.

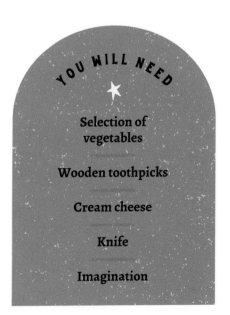

YOU WILL NEED

Selection of vegetables

Wooden toothpicks

Cream cheese

Knife

Imagination

If you want your creation to last, avoid squishy foods like grapes and tomatoes. Hard vegetables like potatoes and carrots take much longer to degrade.

Build your animal. Use wooden toothpicks to attach different body parts together, and cream cheese to 'glue' on any small features, like eyes or teeth. Sculpt different body parts and cut them in to shapes. Be creative. It's great to build cats and dogs, but can you build something more unusual like a Stegosaurus or an octopus?

How easy was it to find fruit and vegetables to use? Take a photo of your creation then eat your animal! Any fruit can be guzzled directly, whilst any vegetables can be turned into soup. Ask a grown-up to help you with this. Don't let your vegetable animal rot away on a bedroom shelf. What a waste that would be!

Make this an engineering challenge by trying to build the tallest free-standing animal that you can.

Try the same task again three months later when the season has changed. What can you make this time? As different ingredients become available, you may find that your inspiration changes.

ROOT-GROWTH VIEWER

Plant roots always grow in the direction of gravity. This is called gravitropism (or geotropism). Watch gravitropism in action by building a root-growth viewer from an old CD case.

YOU WILL NEED

★

Old CD case

Bowl

Soil and water

Beans

Sticky tape

Eyedropper

Permanent marker

Find an unwanted CD case that is made entirely of transparent plastic. Open up the CD case and remove the plastic tray that usually holds the CD. This can be discarded.

Place a large handful of soil in a bowl. Crumble the soil with your fingers to get rid of any big lumps. Mix the soil with a little water so that it is moist but not too soggy.

Half-fill the CD case with the damp soil, leaving the half closest to the hinge empty. This will give your bean room to grow.

Place the bean in the middle of the soil then sprinkle it with water. Runner beans and broad beans work well. Close the CD case and stand it upright so the hinge is at the top. Tape around the sides of the case but do not tape up the gap in the hinge. This will provide the plant with air and an escape route for the shoot when it becomes too big for the case.

★ Prop up the CD case on a sunny windowsill. Water the bean daily using an eyedropper or syringe. Add a few drops of water through the gap in the hinge.

★ Look at your seed every day. As the seed starts to grow, mark its growth on the CD case using a permanent marker. Label the seed coat, roots, shoots and leaves. What happens to the seed coat as the plant gets bigger? It should begin to shrivel as all the food reserves that are inside become used up by the growing bean plant.

★ The roots will be growing down. When the roots are around 5cm (2in) long, turn the CD case through 90 degrees and prop it back up on the windowsill. The roots will now be pointing in the wrong direction, but watch what happens to the roots over the next few days. They will re-orient and start growing in the direction of gravity. Draw a picture of your results in your science journal.

DID YOU KNOW?
In space, there is very little gravity but plants can still grow. Scientists have grown cress on board the International Space Station.

SENSORY GARDEN TEST

Gardens can be so much more than just grass and hedges. With a little thought, it's possible to create an area that stimulates all of the senses. Test your senses with a homegrown sensory garden.

★ Find a little bit of garden where you are allowed to grow things. If you don't have a garden, you can grow a sensory garden in a large pot or window box.

★ This activity is all about choosing plants that tickle the senses in different ways. You are looking for plants that will give you something to touch, taste, hear, smell and see. To keep costs down, choose plants that can be grown easily from seed, or ask friends for cuttings of plants they already have.

★ Texture is easy to find. Leaves vary a lot, from rough to smooth, and furry to spiky. Plant something you will enjoy touching like the lamb's ear shown opposite.

These are small silvery plants with soft velvety leaves that feel just like lambs' ears.

YOU WILL NEED
★

A little bit of garden

Seeds and plants

Trowel

Water

Sunshine!

Herbs are tasty plants. Sow basil or chives from seed. They grow quickly and are a welcome addition to many recipes. Alternatively, you could grow vegetables to tickle your taste buds. Lettuces, peas and carrots are all fast and easy to grow.

It's not easy to find plants that make a noise, but they do exist. Tall grasses make a whispering noise when the wind blows through them. Sweetcorn and bamboo also grow big and tall. Listen carefully and you'll hear them rustle on a windy day.

Many plants are strongly scented. Some smells help to attract pollinators, whilst others act to deter predators. Try planting lavender (which smells like lavender), curry plants (which smell like curry) and the wonderful chocolate cosmos flower (which smells like everyone's favourite treat).

After planting for texture, taste, sound and scent, add the plant that you most like to look at. Beauty is in the eye of the beholder, but who doesn't like a sunflower? These jolly giants are easy to grow, stunning to look at, and attract insects and birds to the garden.

DID YOU KNOW?
The corpse flower, which grows in Sumatra, is one of the world's stinkiest flowers. It smells like a rotting corpse but thankfully it only blooms for around 24 hours, once every four to six years. Don't plant one of these in your garden!

Record all of the plants that you grow and the senses that you use to enjoy them. Can you tell the plants apart with your eyes shut?

COLOUR-CHANGING FLOWERS

Plants absorb water from the soil then transport it from their roots all the way to their flowers, leaves and shoots. This is called transpiration and you can demonstrate it by keeping a cut white flower in food colouring. Watch what happens to the petals.

YOU WILL NEED

A selection of small vases or glass jars

Water

Food colouring

White cut flowers

Sharp knife

★ Fill the vases with fresh water. If your cut flowers come with plant food, mix up a jug of water with plant food and then fill the vases with the mixture.

★ Add a few drops of food colouring to each vase so the water changes colour. Gel food colourings tend to work better than natural food colourings, and darker colours like red and green tend to work better than lighter colours, like yellow and orange. Make the water in each vase a different colour.

You can see when the coloured water reaches the flower because the flower starts to change colour. This can happen quite quickly. Chrysanthemums start to change colour in just half an hour. They look stripy. This is the food colouring inside the xylem tubes in the flower.

Let the experiment run for a week or more. Change the water every few days. Every time you do this, cut another 1cm (½in) off the stem of each flower. This helps to keep the liquid flowing through the plant. Take a photo of the results. How bright are your flowers?

Trim about 1cm (½in) off the stem of each flower before putting a single flower into each vase. You can use any cut white flower, but roses, chrysanthemums and carnations (shown here) all work well.

Place the vases on a table or shelf and watch what happens. Cut flowers have no roots, so instead, the water is drawn into the plants' stem. The stem is full of tiny tubes that are made from a plant tissue called xylem. The water flows through the tubes all the way to the flower.

GROW YOUR NAME

Cress is simple and fun to grow. The tiny seeds contain everything that the plants need to germinate. Grow your name in cress, then eat the results!

⭐ You will need as many paper towels as there are letters in your name. If your name is Helen, for example, you will need five paper towels. If your name is Joe, you will need three. Spread out the paper towels on the tray. If they don't fit, fold them in half.

⭐ Write your name on the towels in big letters. Write one letter per towel, so your name is spread across the tray. Spray the towels with water so they are damp. Don't over-water the towels or they will fall apart.

⭐ Carefully sprinkle the cress seeds over the letters of your name. Press them lightly into the paper towels using your fingers. Take care not to spill any seeds in the area around your name. Place the tray in a sunny indoor spot, like a windowsill.

Water the seeds regularly using the sprayer. Make sure the paper towels don't dry out. If it's warm, you may need to water the seeds twice a day.

The seeds should sprout quickly, within a day or two. About one week later, the plants should be full-grown. Place the tray on the ground and take a photo of your handiwork from above. How does your name look?

DID YOU KNOW?
Cress seeds can be eaten too. They're extra delicious when baked or toasted.

When you're done, use scissors to trim the cress and eat the green clippings. Cress is packed full of vitamin C and minerals like potassium and iron. It has a mild, peppery taste and makes a great addition to sandwiches, salads and soups.

If you let the cress grow until it's around 7cm (2¹/₂in) tall or taller, then it should grow back when you cut it. This means that your name will reappear in all of its green glory. You'll be able to do this a couple of times before the plant goes straggly and starts to make seeds rather than leaves.

GROW PLANTS FROM FOOD SCRAPS

Plants have such a strong urge to grow, that some plants we eat will keep on growing from the parts that we throw away. Some of them will even grow into complete new plants you can eat! See which ones you can grow on the windowsill.

YOU WILL NEED

★

Glass jars

Plates or saucers

Fresh water

Food scraps:
carrot tops, onion bases,
celery or lettuce bases,
leafy herb leaves

★ For root vegetables like carrots and beetroot, you want to keep the top of the root (where the leaves attach to the vegetable), and a little bit of the root itself. To get them to grow, put them onto a saucer of water. Check every day and add more water to the saucer as it dries out. In a few days you should see fresh green leaves growing. You can eat them.

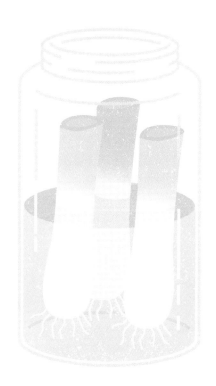

Plants are very different from animals, because they can often regrow after being cut in half. They need air, water and sunlight to regrow, but they will eventually run out of nutrients unless they're planted in soil.

Beetroot leaves have a mild flavour and make a nice salad. Carrot leaves can be a bit bitter, so you may not like them.

For onions, you want the base of the bulb (where the roots stick out). You can use the bottom of spring (green) onions, or bulb onions, it doesn't matter. Pop them into the bottom of a glass jar with some water. Check on them every day and replace the old water with fresh water. Very soon you will see new roots growing from the onion base, and you may start to see fresh green leaves as well. The leaves are edible, just like chives.

You can regrow leafy greens that grow from a solid section (called a 'heart'), like cabbage, lettuce and celery. We often throw that part away because it's tough, but if you put it onto a saucer of water and keep checking on it every day, you should find that it starts to grow new roots and fresh, edible leaves.

You can also try growing the leaves themselves. Leafy greens, and leafy herbs like parsley, coriander and watercress will often grow roots in a jar of water. If you want to, you can then pot them up into soil and they will continue to grow into larger plants.

SEED BOMBS

Welcome wildlife into your garden by creating new habitats full of wild flowers and grasses. Make bombs filled with wild seeds then launch them at a bare patch of earth.

YOU WILL NEED

★

Wildflower seeds

Compost

Powdered clay

Mixing bowl

Water

★ This is an activity for spring or early summer, when the ground is soft and there is plenty of rainfall. Collect some wildflower seeds. These can either be seeds that you harvest from wildflowers growing in the garden, or packets of seeds bought from the shops.

★ Think about the place where you want the seeds to grow. Is it shady or sunny? Different plants like to grow in different places, so choose a combination of seeds that will grow well in the site you have selected.

★ Prepare the bombs. Add one handful of seeds, three handfuls of clay and five handfuls of compost to the mixing bowl. Powdered clay can be bought from craft shops, but some gardens have soil that already contains a lot of clay. You can tell if your soil is clay rich by testing its texture (see pages 74–5) or just by feeling it. Clay soil is sticky. It doesn't crumble easily and can be very difficult to dig! If you have clay soil in your garden, use a slightly different recipe. Use one handful of seeds, five handfuls of clay soil and two handfuls of compost.

It's time to get your hands dirty. Mix up all of the ingredients in the bowl then add some water, a little bit at time, until the mixture becomes sticky. Break off handfuls of the mixture and mould it into balls using your hands. Place the balls somewhere warm, like a windowsill, and leave them to dry overnight.

DID YOU KNOW?
Some birds drop seed bombs of their own when they eat seeds and then poo them out!

Now for the fun bit! 'Plant' the seeds by lobbing the bombs at bare patches of earth in the garden. Ideally, the seed bombs should be detonated the day before rain is forecast. A little water will help to give the seeds a head start.

See how high or far you can throw your seed bombs before they explode, then sit back and watch the plants grow. Make a note of your successes in your science journal.

SPEEDY SEEDS

Seeds germinate too slowly to watch in real time, but when the process is recorded and speeded up, the seeds seem to come to life. Make a time-lapse film of seeds germinating and watch as the shoots reach for the sky.

YOU WILL NEED

Transparent plastic cup

Scissors

Soil

Sunflower seeds

Water

Smartphone with camera

Small tripod

Plug-in light (optional)

⭐ Create a couple of drainage holes in the bottom of the clear plastic cup by pushing the tip of the scissors through the base. Half-fill the cup with soil. Carefully place a couple of sunflower seeds at the edges of the pot, and cover them lightly with 1cm (½in) of soil. Make sure the seeds are still visible through the side of the cup. Water the soil lightly.

⭐ Get ready to make your time-lapse video. All videos are made up of fast-changing pictures or 'frames'. In order for our brains to perceive these pictures as moving, they need to be played back at a certain speed. Most videos play at least twenty-four frames per second.

Time-lapse videos still play twenty-four frames per second, but all of the frames are recorded separately with a gap between them. So, a film-maker may take one picture, wait for 5 minutes, take another picture, wait for 5 minutes, take another picture and so on.

This can be very time-consuming! Fortunately, most smartphones and digital cameras have a built-in time-lapse function. This means you can set the camera up and then leave it to take the pictures for you.

Set up your experiment somewhere light and bright, like a windowsill. It's really important that the camera doesn't move or wobble during the filming, so it needs to be mounted on a tripod. Put the plant and the tripod on the

If you're inspired by this experiment, try taking a time-lapse film of a flower opening.

windowsill, then adjust the height of the tripod so the camera is level with the seed.

The sunflower seed should be in the middle of the picture with plenty of space all around it. That way, when the roots and shoots emerge, you'll be able to record them growing. Make sure the shot is in focus, then start recording. Don't forget to water the sunflower as needed.

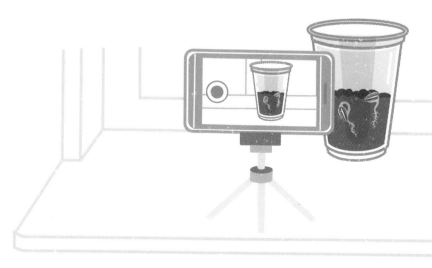

GROW A MINI GARDEN

Many people don't have a big outdoor garden of their own, but it doesn't matter. It can be fun to grow your own mini garden in a seed tray. See what mini things you can manage to grow.

YOU WILL NEED

Paper and pens

Seed tray

Compost

Mini plants

Moss

Sticks, pebbles and craft items

When professional gardeners are making a new garden, they don't just turn up and start digging. They begin by designing their garden with a pen and paper. Think about what sort of miniature garden you'd like to create. It could be a regular family garden with grass and a patio, or it could be something different. Perhaps you could make a wildlife garden, or a prehistoric garden full of dinosaurs. Plan your design on paper and think about how you will create the different features that you want to include. Remember it all has to fit inside a seed tray.

When you are ready to begin, fill the seed tray with compost. Make sure the compost is level and water it lightly. Following the plan, add in your features. Gravel can be used to make paths, lids can be used to make ponds, and twigs can be used to make fences or wigwams.

If you're feeling adventurous, you could include a larger structure like a shed or a stream.

The plants also need to be mini. Grow mini trees from seed or take cuttings from living plants and push them into the soil. Slice the top off a carrot or a parsnip and place it in water (see pages 112–13). In a few days it will have sprouted in to a 'tree' that you can include in your garden.

To create a lawn, sow grass seeds directly onto the compost. If you want a faster alternative, collect moss and press it into the soil. Hey presto, instant grass! Add in plants with tiny flowers like daisies or forget-me-nots.

If you want to make it extra realistic, make mini birds and tiny insects from modelling clay and then put them in. Perhaps there could be chickens in the garden or fish in the pond? What else can you include in your miniature garden?

The miniature garden is alive, so remember to water it regularly and give it a trim when the plants get too big.

SOW STORE-CUPBOARD SEEDS

Our kitchen cupboards are full of dried seeds that we use for cooking and flavouring dishes. It's easy to forget that these ingredients are plants that can still grow with a little help. Rummage through your kitchen cupboards and sow some store-cupboard seeds. Which ones grow the best?

⭐ Take a look through your kitchen cupboards and find some dried seeds. Tinned items that have been pre-cooked won't grow, but dried seeds, which usually come in plastic bags or cardboard packaging, should work well.

⭐ See how many different types of seed you can find. Sometimes these seeds are sold as single ingredients. You may, for example, find packets of dried chickpeas, popping corn, lentils, mung beans, buckwheat and barley. Sometimes these items

YOU WILL NEED

Store-cupboard seeds

Paper towels

Tray

Water

Plant pots

Compost

come all mixed up. Some retailers sell mixed packets of seeds which people use to make soups.

Check the packaging to make sure the dried seeds are not 'split'. Split lentils, for example, are lentils that have literally been split in half. These will not germinate.

The seeds have been dried out to help preserve them. Many store-cupboard seeds will germinate but they need to be rehydrated first. Lay out some paper towels on a tray. Moisten the towels with water. Place five or six of each of the different seeds onto the towels, then cover the seeds with a second layer of paper towels. Moisten the top layer of paper towels with water. Place the tray somewhere warm.

The different seeds will rehydrate and germinate at different rates, so check the seeds every couple of days. They need to be kept moist whilst they are germinating, so keep sprinkling the towels with water.

When the shoots start to appear, transfer the seeds into plant pots. Fill the pots with compost and gently place the seedlings on top. Sprinkle a little more compost on top but make sure that the shoots are poking through. Water the plants regularly and keep a record of which seeds germinate successfully. In time, you will have a windowsill full of crops.

LEAF RUBBING

**Leaves come in all different shapes and sizes.
See how many different leaves you can find and
make your own indoor tree out of the
leaf rubbings you make.**

⭐ Collect as many different leaves as you can find. What trees are there in your garden? Are there different trees in the local park? Gather a variety of leaves in different shapes and sizes. This is an activity for spring, summer or early autumn, when there are leaves on the trees. Fallen leaves can be used to make rubbings as long as they are still fresh and firm.

⭐ Place one of the leaves onto the book. (The book is just there to provide a hard, smooth background surface.) Make sure the smooth side of the leaf is facing down, and the veins on the underside of the leaf are facing up.

⭐ Cover the leaf with a piece of white paper. Weigh the paper down by placing a couple of heavy pebbles at the edges. This will help to stop the paper from moving whilst you are doing your rubbing.

DID YOU KNOW?
The world's longest leaves belong to a palm tree called Raphia regalis. Each leaf can be over 3m (10ft) wide and 24m (78ft) long, but the structure is subdivided into around 180 separate leaflets.

Lots of leaves!

**A big book
(any will do)**

Paper

**A couple of
heavy pebbles**

**Coloured crayons
or soft pencils**

Adhesive putty

Go outside and feel some tree trunks. Find a tree with a textured trunk. Carefully hold a piece of paper over the trunk and make a rubbing of it. You'll need to repeat this several times in order to make a long tree trunk.

Assemble your tree. Find a bare wall that needs livening up, but check with a grown-up first. Start by sticking on the trunk, then arrange the leaves to complete the tree.

Grab your crayons or pencils and lightly rub around the outline of the leaf. You should see the shape of the leaf on the paper. Now rub over the inside of the leaf, taking care to highlight the veins and patterns that emerge.

Make lots of leaf rubbings, using different colours and different leaves. Cut the leaves out and put them to one side. Now it's time to make the tree trunk.

HOW TALL IS YOUR TREE?

You don't need a tall ladder to measure the height of a tall tree. It may sound odd, but a simple way to do this involves bending over and sticking your head between your legs. Give it a try and find out how tall the trees in your garden are.

★ Find the tree that you want to measure. Stand with your back to the tree, then walk forwards a couple of paces. Keeping your legs straight, bend down and look at the tree through your legs. Can you see the top of the tree?

★ If you can't, move backwards or forwards until the top of the tree is visible. Mark the spot by scuffing the ground with your shoe then use the tape measure to record the distance between the mark and the base of the tree.

★ The tree is the same height as this measurement. So, for example, if the tape measure records a distance of 6m (20ft), the tree is also 6m (20ft) tall.

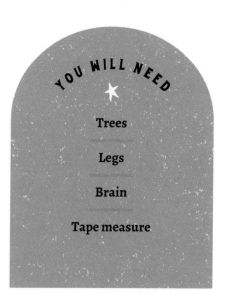

YOU WILL NEED

★

Trees

Legs

Brain

Tape measure

The method works because of a clever bit of maths. When you can see the top of the tree through your legs, the angle between the ground and the top of the tree is approximately 45 degrees. Trees grow up in a straight line, so the angle between the ground and the tree trunk is 90 degrees.

Now think triangles. Imagine a triangle that goes from the base of the tree to its top, to your mark on the ground, and back to the base.

The angles in a triangle always add up to 180 degrees, so the third angle in the triangle must also be 45 degrees. This makes the triangle isosceles. Isosceles triangles have two equal sides, so this means that the distance between you and the tree is about the same as the height of the tree itself.

What is the height of the largest tree you can find? This method also works with other tall things like houses, pylons and giraffes, so why not try measuring other tall objects? Just don't get too close to a giraffe!

45°   90°

GROW A GRASSY MONSTER

Have you ever wondered what it would be like to have your very own pet monster? Here's a chance to find out. Create a monster with real, growing hair. Make it as ugly as you can.

YOU WILL NEED

★

Pair of nylon tights

Grass seed

Sawdust

Elastic band

Yogurt pot

Pens, paints, paper and glue

Plastic googly eyes (optional)

Cardboard

★ Cut the foot off an old pair of nylon tights to make a short sock. Fill the toe of the sock with grass seed. Top up the sock with sawdust so it forms a ball shape. This will be the monster's head. Monsters aren't pretty, so the head doesn't need to be perfect. If it's lumpy and bumpy it will make your monster even more monstrous. Use the elastic band to close the sock shut so the monster's brains can't fall out.

★ Decorate the yogurt pot. This will be the monster's body. Give the monster arms and legs, and maybe even a tail. What does the body look like? Is your monster covered in scales or spots? Is it wearing clothes or is it naked?

Fill up the yogurt pot with water and balance the monster's head on the body. Carefully glue some googly eyes and teeth onto the monster. If you don't have plastic googly eyes, you can make some eyes out of cardboard. How many eyes does your monster have? Just two? Some spiders have eight eyes, so you could add more.

Place your monster somewhere light and sunny, like a windowsill. Top up the water from time to time. The bottom of the monster's head should always be touching the water. The water will soak up through the sawdust and help the grass seeds to germinate.

A few weeks later, your monster should be sporting a fine head of spiky grass hair. Try styling the hair. Would your monster look good with bunches, or should you trim the grass around the sides of the head and give it a Mohican? Take a photo of your creation and put it in your journal. See how long the grass can grow, then when you are ready, cut it all off and start again.

LEAF SKELETONS

Humans have skeletons made of bone. Leaves have skeletons made of hollow vascular tubes. Boil away the fleshy parts of the leaf to reveal its intricate inner skeleton.

YOU WILL NEED

Leaves

Five cups of water

One cup of sodium carbonate

Old saucepan

Water

Bowl

Washing-up gloves

Tweezers

Kitchen towel

Small stiff brush

Choose some leaves. Thick, waxy, glossy leaves like magnolia and holly work well, but take longer to prepare. Thinner, duller deciduous leaves like beech and oak also work well, and are quicker to prepare.

Ask an adult to do the first part of this experiment for you. Add five cups of water and one cup of sodium carbonate to the saucepan. Sodium carbonate is also known as washing soda or soda ash. It can irritate the skin, so be careful. Heat the mixture gently until the sodium carbonate has dissolved.

Using the tweezers, add the leaves to the mixture. Make sure they are fully immersed in the liquid. Allow the leaves to simmer for half an hour until they are soft and bendy. If you are preparing waxy leaves, they will need to simmer for an extra 30 minutes.

✳ Prepare a bowl containing only water. Using the tweezers, transfer the leaves from the saucepan to the bowl. Let the leaves sit in the water for 10 minutes. This softens the leaves further and helps to wash away the sodium carbonate.

✳ Remove the leaves from the water and place them on a piece of kitchen towel.

✳ Politely ask the grown-up to stop interfering. Now it's your turn. Put on some washing-up gloves to protect your skin. The leaves should be soft and starting to deteriorate. Use a small stiff brush to tease away the fleshy parts of the leaf that surround the skeleton.

Sometimes leaf skeletons occur naturally when microbes in the soil eat away at the fleshy parts of the leaf.

This is delicate work. Be careful not to break the skeleton or the leaf. If the flesh doesn't come away easily, soak the leaf in water for another 30 minutes, then try again.

✳ Transfer the leaf to a new piece of kitchen towel and allow it to dry. You now have your leaf skeleton. Look at the intricate network of vessels that transport liquid around the leaf. Take a photo and put it in your journal.

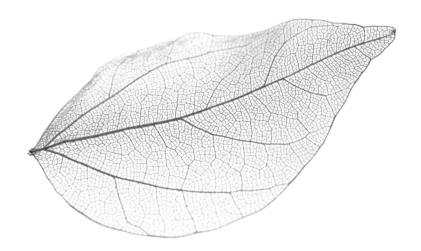

SEED DISPERSAL SPINNER

In autumn, some trees release 'helicopter' seeds that spin through they air as they tumble to earth. Make a paper seed spinner to show how these seeds are dispersed in the wild.

✳ Place the sticky note on the table, sticky side up, and spin it around so the sticky strip is at the bottom. Draw a horizontal line three-quarters of the way down the sticky note. This is the line you will use for folding.

✳ Make two equally spaced cuts that go from the top of the sticky note down to the folding line. This divides the top of the sticky note into three equal strips.

✳ Fold the middle strip downwards to make a 'Y' shape. It should stick to the sticky part of the sticky note.

✳ The outer strips can now be folded. Fold one strip towards you and the other strip away from you. This time the strips should not stick down. They should flap around freely. These are the 'wings' of the helicopter.

The helicopter needs a little bit of weight, so slide a paper clip on to the middle, downward section of the 'Y' shape. The seed disperser is now good to go.

Stand on a chair. Hold your arm up high, and let it go. How did it fly? Where did it land? What happens if you add more paper clips or change the shape of the wings? Make a note of your findings.

Plants have evolved many different ways to ensure that their seeds are dispersed as widely as possible. This is because if a seed germinates too close to the parent plant, the plants will have to compete with each other for resources, like light and nutrients.

Some seeds are dispersed by animals. Others are dispersed by the wind. Seeds that are transported by wind have some clever adaptations that help to keep them airborne. The wings on your seed disperser help to do this. As the seed disperser falls, the air pushing upwards gives the seed lift. The two arms get a push in opposite directions. This makes it spin.

HOW OLD IS YOUR TREE?

Have you ever wondered how old the trees in your garden are? Most people know that you can estimate a tree's age by counting the number of tree rings it has, but to do this accurately the tree has to be cut down. Try these alternate methods to estimate the age of a tree without damaging it.

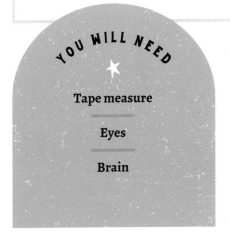

YOU WILL NEED

Tape measure

—

Eyes

—

Brain

If the tree is in your garden or local park, do you or someone else know the year that it was planted? If you do, the task is simple. Subtract the year the tree was planted from the year it is now. This is the tree's age.

As trees grow, they lay down new layers of tissue around the trunk. This tissue forms the rings that some people use to age trees. Every year, as new rings are added, the circumference of the tree increases, so a tree's circumference can be used to help estimate its age.

Stand next to your tree. Measure 1.5m (5ft) up from the base of the tree trunk, then wrap the tape measure around the trunk and record the tree's circumference.

Trees grow at different rates. This depends on many factors, including the amount of rainfall and the availability of nutrients. In gardens and parks, the circumference of broadleaved trees like oak and beech increases by around 2cm (3/4in) every year. To find a rough estimate of the age of your tree, simply divide its circumference by 2 (or 0.75 if measuring in inches).

If the tree is a conifer, there is another method you can use. Conifers are trees that produce cones, such as pines, cedars and firs. Unlike broadleaved trees, many conifers grow in a regular pattern. Every year, a new set of branches grows out from the trunk. They're a bit like the spokes on a bicycle wheel. Whorls are the areas where the branches radiate out from the

What is the oldest tree you can find? The oldest known living tree is over 4,850 years old. It's a Great Basin bristlecone pine that lives in the White Mountains of California. It's called Methuselah, after the long-lived character from the Bible.

trunk, so if you count the number of whorls you will have an idea of the tree's age. Take care not to count any small branches that are growing between the whorls. These are not genuine whorls.

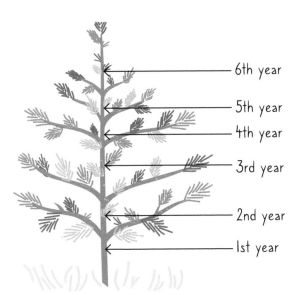

6th year

5th year

4th year

3rd year

2nd year

1st year

WHY DO LEAVES CHANGE COLOUR?

In autumn, the leaves of many trees turn from green to gold, orange and red. We're all familiar with this spectacular transformation, but have you ever wondered why it happens? Find out why leaves change colour using this simple experiment.

YOU WILL NEED

Leaves

Scissors and spoon

Glass jar

Surgical spirit

Bowl and hot water

Coffee filter paper

Sticky tape

Collect a handful of green leaves. The leaves should come from a deciduous tree, like an oak or a maple, which will shed its leaves when autumn comes. Using the scissors, cut the leaves into tiny pieces, then put them in the glass jar. Working outside or in a well-ventilated room, pour in just enough surgical spirit to cover the leaves, then 'mush' the leaves up by pressing them against the sides of the jar with the spoon.

Put the lid on the jam jar. If you don't have a lid, cover it with aluminium foil. Place the jar into a bowl full of hot tap water and leave it for an hour. Every 10 minutes or so, pick up the jar and swirl it around. As the water cools down, replace it with more hot water. Do you notice anything happening to the liquid? The colour should begin to change.

✳ Cut some long thin strips from the coffee filter paper. The strips should be 1–2cm (1⁄2–1in) across, and at least as long as the jar is tall. Take the jar out of the bowl and remove the lid. Dip one end of the strip into the leafy liquid and tape the other end to the outside of the jar so the paper can't fall in. Wait for a couple of hours. What do you see?

There should be at least two different stripes on your filter paper: one green and one yellow or orange. This shows you the different colours that are hiding inside the green leaves, just waiting to burst out in autumn.

✳ Chlorophyll is the green substance that makes plants green, but plants also contain yellow and orange substances that we can't see because they are masked by the green of the chlorophyll.

✳ In autumn, as the days become shorter, trees stop producing chlorophyll and any chlorophyll that is left in the leaves is broken down. The green colour fades, so the yellow and orange colours can finally be seen.

WATCH PLANTS BREATHE

Animals aren't the only things that breathe. Plants are living things and they breathe, too. Just like us, they 'breathe in' one sort of gas, and then 'exhale' another. Watch this process happen with this simple experiment.

YOU WILL NEED

★

Large glass bowl

Water

Large leaf

Scissors

Stone

Magnifying glass (if you have one)

★ Fill the large glass bowl with warm water from a tap. Glass bowls are great for this experiment because they let you watch what's happening from all angles, and slightly magnify the contents of the bowl. If you don't have a glass bowl, any bowl will do.

★ Head into the garden and find a leaf. It needs to be alive, so it should be fresh from a tree or other plant. The bigger the better. Choose the largest leaf you can find, then snip it at the stem and bring it inside.

★ Place the leaf inside the bowl of water and weigh it down with the stone. The leaf should be completely underwater. Place the bowl somewhere sunny. This could be outside in the sunshine, or inside on a windowsill. Now for the hardest bit. You need to wait. Let the experiment run for a couple of hours.

When you return to the experiment, take a look at the leaf. If you have a magnifying glass, use it to look at the leaf closely. What do you see?

The leaf should be covered in lots of tiny bubbles. Poke the leaf gently with your finger and the bubbles should rise to the surface.

When we breathe, we breathe in a gas called oxygen, and breathe out a gas called carbon dioxide. Plants are different. They absorb carbon dioxide and water and convert it into sugars and oxygen. This is called photosynthesis and it's powered by sunshine.

When we breathe, we use our lungs. When plants breathe, they use tiny holes in their leaves called stomata. The little bubbles that you can see are bubbles of oxygen that are escaping from the stomata in the leaves.

HOW TO GROW PLANTS IN SPACE

In the future, when humans travel to Mars or other faraway planets, they'll need to be able to grow their own food – but soil is heavy and floats around in space! So, scientists are planning ahead and growing plants without soil. This is called hydroponics. Grow your own space plants by sowing seeds soil-free.

YOU WILL NEED

Large plastic bottle

Scissors and string

Cotton wool balls

Water

Bean seeds

Modelling clay

Wooden skewers

Remove the lid from the large plastic bottle. Using scissors, carefully cut the bottle in half. Take the top half and turn it upside down, then place it into the bottom half of the bottle. This is where the seeds will go.

Using the top part as a funnel, fill the bottom part of the bottle with water. The water level should be just below the upside-down neck of the bottle.

Cut five long pieces of string. They should be at least three times as long as the height of your hydroponic planter. Feed the pieces of string down through the neck of the bottle so they dangle in the water. Don't push too much string through the neck of the bottle or it will all fall through. Most of the string will be all tangled up inside the upside-down top half of the bottle. This is just fine.

⭐ Put five or six cotton wool balls on top of the tangled string, and sprinkle a handful of bean seeds on top of the cotton wool.

⭐ Make a tripod to support the growing seeds. This is a bit fiddly. Make three little blobs of modelling clay and arrange them into a small triangle shape on a table. Press one skewer into each blob, then use another small piece of string to tie the other ends of the skewers together. The structure should look like a little tepee. Now balance the tripod on top of the cotton wool, and move the planter into a bright sunny place. Watch to see what happens.

⭐ The water will soak up through the string and into the cotton wool. After a few days, the seeds will germinate. The roots will grow down through the neck of the bottle into the water, and the shoots will grow up and around the tripod.

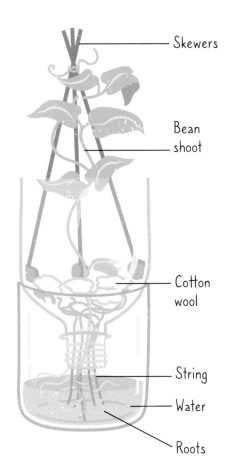

Skewers

Bean shoot

Cotton wool

String

Water

Roots

After a while the seedlings will need extra nutrients. You can buy hydroponic food online, but if you have a fish tank, pond or nearby lake, you could try using some of the water from that.

MAKE A MINI GREENHOUSE

Greenhouses help plants to thrive, but just how much of a difference do they really make? Make a mini greenhouse from old CDs and see how temperature affects plant growth.

YOU WILL NEED

Three clear CD cases

Clear sticky tape

Sweet pepper seeds

Two small plant pots

Soil

Thermometer and ruler

Open up the CD cases and remove the plastic tray that usually holds the CD. This can be recycled with the plastic waste. The first two CD cases will form the four walls of the greenhouse. Open up the cases so the hinges are at 90 degrees. Stand the two cases up and arrange them so they form a box. Stick the cases together using sticky tape. At this stage the box has no bottom and no top.

The third CD case is going to form the roof of the mini greenhouse and reinforce one of the walls. Open up the third CD case. Position it so that one side of the case rests on one of the walls to form an additional wall panel (it's a bit like double glazing), and the other side of the case forms a horizontal roof. Stick the new wall panel to the structure using tape, but take care not to stick the roof down. Often gardeners ventilate their greenhouses by letting a little air in. This will enable you to do the same.

The greenhouse is now ready to go. Fill the two pots with soil. Add a couple of sweet pepper seeds to each of the pots and sprinkle a little extra soil on top. Water the seeds so the soil becomes moist. Put the two pots on a windowsill but cover one with the mini greenhouse. Place the thermometer inside the greenhouse.

Now watch and wait for the peppers to grow. Give the seedlings a little water every other day, or whenever the soil is close to drying out. Which seedling germinates first? When the seeds have germinated measure how quickly they grow. Use a ruler to measure their height twice a week. Measure the temperature inside the greenhouse, then remove the thermometer and measure the temperature outside the greenhouse. Record your observations in your science journal.

Greenhouses keep plants warm, even in the depths of winter. The glass (or plastic) traps the sun's heat so sometimes the temperature inside the greenhouse can be more than 10°C (18°F) warmer than the outside temperature.

MAKE AN ECOSYSTEM IN A JAR

Plants use the carbon dioxide we exhale to help make the oxygen that we breathe. Demonstrate some of the ecological cycles that keep us alive by creating an ecosystem in a jar. See how long you can make the ecosystem last.

YOU WILL NEED

★

Large glass jar

Pebbles and charcoal

Soil and potting compost

Plants

Spoon

Water

Ecosystems are communities of living things and the place where they live. For example, your garden is an ecosystem because it contains living things like birds, insects, bacteria and plants, and physical structures like fences, stones and water.

To build an ecosystem in a jar, first put a layer of pebbles in the base of the jar. This will give any excess water somewhere to collect, so the plants don't drown!

Sprinkle a thin layer of charcoal over the pebbles. You can buy charcoal from a shop or collect it from the ashes of a disused barbecue or bonfire. The charcoal is important because it acts as a filter, helping to collect impurities and keep the ecosystem healthy.

Prepare a mixture that is half soil and half potting compost, and add a thick layer to the jar. Potting compost is good because it contains plenty of nutrients to help the plants grow, and the soil is important because it's packed with bacteria. Together, the three layers should fill about a third of the jar.

Add some small plants. Anything will do, but choose plants that require a similar amount of water. So, for example, a cactus and a daisy will not go well together. The plants should easily fit in the jar with room for growth. Dig a small hole in the soil with a spoon and add the plants. Cover the roots with soil.

As a finishing touch, you could add a bigger pebble in amongst the plants. There's no real reason for this. It just looks professional! Now put the lid on the jar and place it somewhere that is well lit.

The idea is that the ecosystem will look after itself, so there's no need to water it or add in air, but for the first couple of days it may need some assistance. If the soil looks dry, add a little water. If the inside of the jar is always covered in condensation, then open the lid to let it breathe for a while.

Take a photo of your ecosystem and stick it in your journal. Record how long the ecosystem lasts before the plants start to die.

SMART PLANTS

Some people talk to their plants because they think it helps the plants to grow, but did you know that plants are very good at communicating? They may not have mouths to talk with, or ears to hear with, but plants are constantly sending out and receiving information.

★ If a flowering plant wants to attract the attention of a pollinating insect, for example, it may release chemicals into the air. There is a plant that grows in Sumatra called the titan arum or 'corpse flower' (right). It releases a chemical

called dimethyl trisulfide, which smells like rotting flesh. Flesh-eating insects, like some beetles and flies, find the smell irresistible, so they visit the flower, pick up its pollen and then spread it around the neighbourhood when they finally buzz off. The corpse flower might not talk out loud, but it is still communicating with a different species.

✱ Plants can also communicate with each other. When bean plants are attacked by leaf-eating flies, they release chemicals into the air that warn the plants' neighbours of an impending attack. In return, the neighbours release different chemicals that repel plant-eating flies and attract fly-eating wasps.

✱ Plants also communicate with each other underground. If one plant is struggling because it has no water, it sends a message via its roots, to plants that are nearby. The neighbours respond by closing tiny pores, called stomata, that normally allow water to evaporate from their leaves. This helps the plant to retain the water that it already has, and prepares it for the future drought.

✱ The more researchers study plants, the more they realise that plants have complex social lives. Trees, for example, can recognise plants that are closely related to them. Sometimes they grow their roots towards their young so they can transfer sugar to them and help them grow. Other times they stop growing their roots towards their young to prevent competition between 'parent' and 'child'.

✱ Plants are social and plants are smart. Did you know that some plants can even count? The Venus flytrap (above) catches insects inside modified leaves that can quickly snap shut. The leaves have specialised trigger hairs that sense the insects, but the trap only shuts if the hairs are touched twice within a period of 10 seconds or so. It then takes a further three touches, when the insect is struggling, for the plant to start producing enzymes that digest the insect. So, the Venus flytrap is doubly smart because it can count at least two things: time and the number of touches.

KITCHEN SINK SCIENCE

It's great being in the garden, but sometimes it's hard to get outside. When it's rainy or cold, you can bring the joys of the garden into the house by performing some kitchen sink science experiments indoors. Kitchen sink science is all about creativity and innovation, and it is inspired by the natural world. Who says you need to leave the house to enjoy the great outdoors?

KITCHEN SINK SCIENCE

The experiments in this section draw their inspiration from the garden and the natural world. They all use natural items, like potatoes, sticks and lavender, which can either be grown or found in the garden. Some of the more exotic ingredients, like avocados and lemons, can be bought from a supermarket or borrowed from a fruit bowl.

Most of the experiments aren't actually done in the kitchen sink (one of them is), but some of them do involve washing-up. My children try to persuade me that washing-up is a grown-up job, so you may want to see if you can pull off the same scam!

The experiments in this section are creative and diverse. In this part of the book, you'll be making lots of 'ometers'. There's a barometer to predict the weather, a thermometer to record the temperature, and an anemometer to measure wind speed. After that, the national weather forecasters had better watch out, as you could be after their jobs.

Go one step further and you could even make some weather. There's a really great experiment to make a cloud in a jar, and another to make a tornado in a bottle. Best of all, you won't get soaked, and along the way you'll learn a little about how the weather works.

There's lots of other fun things to try. Decorate your windows with cardboard silhouettes to stop garden birds from flying into them. Make a pond-dipping net so you can go outside when the rain stops and have an adventure.

Liven up your garden walls (literally) by making a living, breathing, moss-based paint that you can use outside. Eco-graffiti, as it's called, is non-toxic and environmentally friendly, and if you're any good at art – which I'm sure you are – the results are lovely to look at.

By the end of this section, you'll be washing with conker soap, bathing in homemade bath bombs, and relaxing with scented lavender bags. Experiment with the natural ingredients that surround you and see if you can come up with your own kitchen sink science experiments.

TURN POTATOES INTO SLIME

Potatoes may seem ordinary, but they're anything but. Learn about weird materials by making a spud-based substance that is solid when you play with it and liquid when you leave it alone.

Grab a bag full of potatoes and give them a wash. Cut them up as small as possible and place the pieces in a large bowl. Cover the potato pieces in hot water and use the wooden spoon to stir the mixture for 5 minutes. Keep the mixture moving. Do not let the water stand still. What do you see? The water may start to change colour. This is normal.

Acting quickly, strain the potato mixture through the sieve, pouring the liquid into a second large bowl. You don't need the potato chunks now but it's a shame to throw them away, so ask an adult to turn them into something delicious.

Meanwhile, allow the freshly sieved potato water to settle in the new bowl. Do not stir it or disturb it in any way. Leave it for at least 15 minutes. Now what do you see? The mixture should start to separate.

Pour away the upper layer, leaving the thick, white lower layer behind. This is your slime, but it's still a bit dirty so it needs to be washed.

The potato slime isn't a solid, but it's not a liquid either. It's something called a non-Newtonian fluid. Non-Newtonian fluids are weird. They go solid when they are under pressure, but they liquefy when the pressure is removed.

Mix the slime with cold water and transfer it to a glass jar. Put the lid on and shake the mixture vigorously. Leave it to settle for 10 minutes. The white bottom layer will reappear. Quickly pour away the top layer of liquid, and there you have it: your very own potato slime.

Take the milky mixture out and knead it with your fingers. The more you manipulate it, the more dough-like it should become. Try punching it and the mixture should resist. Now what happens when you stop handling it? The semi-solid mixture should 'melt'. It will turn into a liquid and slide through your fingers. Messy, isn't it?

YOU WILL NEED

★

Potatoes

Two large bowls

Knife

Hot water

Wooden spoon

Sieve

Glass jar with lid

MAKE RED CABBAGE pH PAPER

Red cabbage is not only good for you, but it also contains a natural pH indicator that changes colour depending on the acidity of the surroundings. Make your own pH paper strips, then test the pH of some liquids from your home and garden.

YOU WILL NEED

Half a red cabbage

Sharp knife and scissors

Boiling water

Heatproof bowl

Jug or jar

Sieve

Coffee filter paper

Household liquids,
e.g. vinegar or laundry
detergent

Using the knife, chop up half a red cabbage into very small pieces. Place it into the heatproof bowl and cover it completely with freshly boiled water. Leave the mixture for 15 minutes. What do you see? The water should begin to change colour as colourful molecules called 'pigments' leak out of the cabbage.

Sieve the mixture to separate the cabbage from the water. It's a shame to waste good food, so ask an adult to cook the cabbage or give it to a guinea pig! Collect the red-purple liquid in a jug or jar. This is your pH indicator.

After a few hours, remove the strips and allow them to dry. You can hang them on a washing line or put them on a radiator or windowsill. Be careful – the colour can run and cause staining.

Now it's time to get testing. Collect the samples that you want to analyse. Vinegar, lemon juice and laundry detergent all give a good response. Place a drop of the sample onto the pH paper. If the paper becomes a blue, green or yellow colour, the sample is alkaline. If the paper becomes a dark red or purple, the sample is acidic. Record your results in your science journal.

Remember, pH is measured on a scale of 1 to 14. Liquids with a pH of less than 7 are acidic. Liquids with a pH of more than 7 are alkaline. Your pH indicator will have a neutral pH of about 7. Its exact colour will depend on the pH of the water you used.

Prepare the pH paper. Cut the coffee filter paper into small strips that are about 5cm (2in) long and 1cm (1/2in) wide. Place the strips into the pH indicator and leave them to soak. The strips should be completely immersed in the liquid.

You can work out the pH of your sample by comparing the colour of the pH paper against the colour chart on this page.

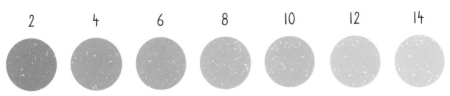

2   4   6   8   10   12   14

DYE IT WITH AVOCADO

Kitchens and gardens are full of plants containing natural chemicals that can be used to dye fabrics. Make a dye from avocado stones, then see if you can make different coloured dyes from different plants.

Four avocado stones

Plastic bag

Breadboard

Hammer

Old saucepan, water

Sieve, wooden spoon

Old blouse or T-shirt, pillowcase or sheet

Put the avocado stones inside the plastic bag and place it on the breadboard. Take the hammer and give the stones a gentle whack. The idea is to break the stones in half and then smash them into smaller pieces. The bag is there for protection as it stops bits of avocado from flying all over the place.

Put the small, freshly crushed avocado pieces into an old saucepan and add 1 litre (1.8 pints) of water. Heat the mixture until it begins to boil, then reduce the heat and let it simmer gently for an hour. This will help to draw the dye out of the avocado stone and concentrate the dye. Make sure the pan doesn't

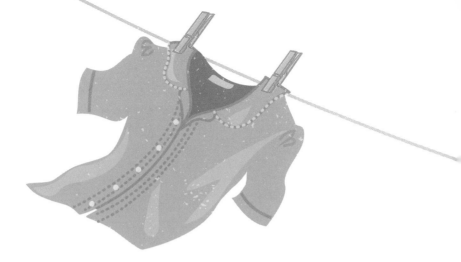

boil dry. Top it up with a little water if needed. Strain the mixture through a sieve and return the liquid to the saucepan.

Prepare the fabric. White cotton works well, so you could use an old blouse or T-shirt, or cut up an old pillowcase or sheet (check with an adult first). Moisten the fabric by running it under a tap, then add it to the saucepan. Make sure the fabric is completely covered. Swirl it around with a spoon and leave it overnight.

The next day, remove the fabric and wring it out. Leave it to dry on a washing line or radiator. When it is dry, ask an adult to iron the fabric on a medium heat. This will help to fix the colour so it won't run when the fabric gets wet.

DID YOU KNOW?
You can also make ink
from avocado stones.
Try using some of the
leftover dye to paint
a picture.

Avocado dye stains fabric a light, rosy pink colour, but what other colours can you make using the natural ingredients that are around you? Experiment with different items from the garden and the kitchen. Onion skins, carrot tops, coffee grounds, blueberries, nettles and pomegranate seeds also make excellent dyes. In your journal, record which items work best.

HELP BIRDS
AVOID WINDOWS

**Birds sometimes fly into windows and injure
or kill themselves. Become a bird hero and help
prevent this from happening by making your
windows bird-proof. The birds will
thank you for it!**

Birds sometimes fly into windows or glass doors because they simply don't see them. The glass acts like a mirror, reflecting images of the trees and the sky, so often the birds don't realise that the glass is actually there.

To prevent birds from flying into windows, the panes need to be made more obvious. This can be achieved simply by hanging objects in front of them.

Small birds are frightened of large predatory birds, like hawks, and will go to great lengths to avoid them. Sketch a picture of a hawk on an A4 piece of card. Its wings should be outstretched as if in

flight. It doesn't need to be a masterpiece, but if you find this difficult, you can print out a picture from the internet and use it as a template.

Colour the hawk in using the black marker pen. The idea is to create a dark silhouette that will be easy for garden birds to spot. Using the scissors, cut the hawk out. Make a small hole in the bird's body, and attach a long piece of cotton thread. Hang the bird in your window using adhesive putty or sticky tape.

Repeat the process. If the window is particularly big, add more than one hawk. Try making a silhouette scene, including trees, flowers, clouds and a sun. Birds are less likely to fly into a window filled with lots of obstacles. Make a note of what happens over time. Is your bird deterrent successful?

DID YOU KNOW?
In some countries, a group of hawks is called a 'kettle' of hawks, but in reality, it's rare to see hawks together. Adult hawks tend to be solitary birds that only come together when they breed or migrate.

This simple measure should greatly reduce the number of collisions that occur, but if you do find a bird that has flown into a window, treat it with care. It may be suffering from concussion or have internal injuries. Place it in a quiet, dark place and leave it for a couple of hours. Hopefully the bird will recover.

AMAZING MOULD EXPERIMENT

The world is full of living things so small they can't be seen with the naked eye. When they grow in vast numbers, they become visible. Watch microscopic mould growing into something big on a slice of bread and learn about the conditions needed to make it grow.

Three slices of
white bread

Three pieces of
kitchen towel

Water

Three clear
plastic bags

Masking tape

If you've ever opened the bread bin and found that the loaf is covered in colourful fuzz, that's mould. Mould is a type of fungus. It grows from spores that blow around in the air, and can be found just about everywhere, including on your skin, in the soil and on work surfaces. Some moulds can make people ill, but most are totally harmless.

Prepare your mould-growing bags. Fold the pieces of kitchen towel into quarters and sprinkle them with water so they are damp but not soaking. Now put one piece of kitchen towel into each of the plastic bags.

Press your hand firmly into each slice of bread so it leaves a handprint in the middle. Some of the spores on your skin will be transferred to the bread. Put one piece of bread into each of the bags so it sits on top of the kitchen towel. Now seal the bags tightly shut using the masking tape.

Label the bags 1, 2, 3. Put the first bag in the fridge. Put the second bag onto a warm, brightly lit windowsill. Put the third bag into a dark kitchen cupboard. Now leave your mould to grow.

Check on the experiment every day. You should see mould beginning to form after a couple of days. After seven to ten days the experiment will be done. Do not open the bag. You can study the mould from the outside.

DID YOU KNOW?
Some moulds can kill bacteria. Penicillin is a common antibiotic that was originally discovered in mould.

Do all of the bags contain mouldy bread? Which contains the most mould? Has it grown in the shape of a hand? What conditions does mould need to grow? Take photos and describe your results in your journal. When you are finished, ask a grown-up to dispose of the experiment in an outside bin.

MAKE A POND DIPPING NET

Pond dipping is a great way to learn about all the creatures that live in your neighbourhood pool of water, but it's hard to do without a net. Make your own pond dipping net then go out and survey some aquatic animals.

YOU WILL NEED

Pair of
nylon tights

Scissors, ruler

Wire coat hanger

Needle and thread

Duct tape

Garden cane

Nylon tights are thin and stretchy. They let water pass through but successfully retain small swimming creatures that would otherwise get away. Make sure your adult has finished with the pair of tights you are going to use, as they will never be wearable again.

Measure down about 15cm (6in) from the crotch of the tights. The crotch is the bit between the two legs. Cut the legs of the tights off at this point. Throw the sock bits away or use them to make a bug sucker (see pages 36–7). Gather what's left of the two legs together and tie them into a tight knot. This is going to form the main part of the net.

Open up the wire coat hanger so it makes a diamond shape. Place the net in the middle of the diamond and fold the waistband over the metal. Fasten the tights to the coat hanger by sewing all the way around. A simple running stitch is good for this. If you need some help, ask an adult.

Straighten the coat hanger hook and secure it to the end of the garden cane using duct tape. Your pond dipping net is ready to go. Check out pages 40–1 to learn how to go pond dipping. If you're lucky, you might catch a Smooth newt like the one pictured above.

If you use an old cotton pillow instead of a pair of tights, you'll be able to make a swoop net, which can be used to catch butterflies. Swoop nets tend to be deeper than pond dipping nets because the butterflies will easily fly out of nets that are too shallow. Swoop nets are so called because you need to swoop them through the air in order to catch the butterfly.

See how many different species you can catch with your pond net or swoop net. Record them in your journal.

MAKE A LAVENDER BAG

Lavender contains aromatic oils that have a relaxing effect. Make a mini lavender bag to help you sleep, then experiment with other herbs to see if you can improve on the scent.

YOU WILL NEED

★

Lavender

Scissors

Breadboard

Rice

Bowl

Cotton fabric

Ribbon, elastic band

Prepare your lavender. Lavender plants flower in the summer. Harvest the flowers as they come into bloom. This is when their scent is strongest. Cut the flowers at the base of the stem then lay them out on a breadboard. Put the cut lavender in a sunny spot, like a windowsill or a conservatory. Leave it for at least a week until the lavender is completely dried out.

You may notice that the flowers begin to fade and lose their brilliant purple colour. This doesn't matter. It's the scent that is important. Check every few days to see if the lavender is dry. The flowers will start to crumble from the stem when they are ready.

Prepare the stuffing for the pillow. In a bowl, mix two parts of lavender to one part of rice. The rice helps bulk out the pillow and make it less flimsy.

Prepare the pillowcase. Cut a circle out of the material. The circle should be about the same size as a CD. Place the fabric circle – right-side down – on a table, then add a handful of the lavender mixture to the middle. Carefully gather up the sides of the circle to make a pouch or bag, then use the elastic band to fasten the bag shut. Tie a colourful ribbon around the elastic band to make the lavender bag look more attractive and professional. Put the bag next to your pillow at night, or use it to freshen up a wardrobe or drawer. It's so much better than the smell of socks!

Lavender smells sweet but so do many other garden plants. Some geranium leaves smell of lemon, and herbs like rosemary and thyme also have pleasant scents. Try making some alternate scent bags using other dried garden plants. Make a note of which smell you like the best.

Lavender plants are covered in oil glands. These are tiny star-shaped hairs that can be found on the leaves, flowers and stems. When you rub the plant between your fingers, the glands release oil, which gives the plant its smell.

POTATO POWER

Make a potato battery and use it to power a calculator. See how long the battery lasts, then try making more powerful batteries from other vegetables and fruits.

★ It's easy to make a potato battery. Bend the copper wire in half and poke the sharp ends into the potato. Touch your tongue on the copper wire. Do you notice anything?

★ Poke the galvanised nail into the potato. The nail and the wire should be close to one another but not touching. Now touch the copper wire and the nail with your tongue. What do you notice?

★ When your tongue touched just the copper wire, you probably didn't notice much, but this time, you might feel a tingle or notice a metallic taste. This is a sign that your battery is working. Potato batteries generate a very small electric current that is harmless, but don't go licking shop-bought batteries as these are more powerful and you may receive a small electric shock.

★ Remove the battery casing from the back of your calculator. Warning! Your calculator may never be the same again so make sure it's an old, inexpensive one that you don't mind destroying!

★ Pop out the battery and, using pliers, carefully detach the red and black wires that are attached to it. If your calculator has a solar panel, this will also need to be disconnected. Cut the wires that connect the solar panel to the calculator.

Now make some batteries using other kitchen items. Citrus fruits, like oranges and lemons, work well, as do pickled gherkins and pickled onions. Which battery powers your calculator for the longest?

★ Connect the battery to the calculator. Using one of the leads, connect the black, negative calculator wire to the nail. Using the other lead, connect the red, positive calculator wire to the copper wire. Turn the calculator over and look at the display screen. Your calculator should now be working.

★ The battery works because electrons, which are tiny, negatively charged particles, are moving around the circuit you have created. The potato is an 'electrolyte'. Electrolytes are substances that help keep electric currents flowing.

ECO-GRAFFITI

Many people don't like normal graffiti because it's done with paint and is hard to remove. Eco-graffiti is graffiti that is made with living, growing plants. It's environmentally friendly and easy to remove. Make some with moss and literally bring a wall to life.

YOU WILL NEED

Moss

Bowl, blender

Two cups of water

Two cups of yogurt

One teaspoon of sugar

Cornflour

Paintbrush

Garden wall

This is an activity to prepare in the kitchen and then do outside. First, collect a big handful of moss. Mosses are small flowerless plants that grow in thick green clumps in shady places like forest floors or tree trunks. There are around 12,000 different species. They have thin simple leaves that are packed full of a green substance called chlorophyll.

Put the moss in a bowl and fill it with water. Give the moss a clean by swirling it around with your fingers. This will get rid of any soil that is still attached to it. Remove the moss from the water and break it into small chunks.

Place the moss in the blender. Add the water, yogurt and sugar. Blitz the mixture until it is completely smooth. You might want to ask an adult to help you with this. Remarkably, this doesn't kill the moss. It just breaks the plant up into lots of tiny pieces.

The mixture should have a paint-like texture. If it's too thick, add a little water. Add a little cornflour if it's too runny. The moss paint is now ready to use.

Ask an adult if you can try your eco-graffiti on an outside surface, like a wall or the side of a shed. Remember, moss grows best in shady places, so avoid painting your design onto a surface that is in full sun. Use a brush to paint your design onto the wall. Why not paint something environmental like a tree or an animal?

Check the eco-graffiti every week. If it takes a while to get going, you may need to add some more paint. If it looks like it's drying out, spray it with water. Take a photo and stick it in your journal. How long can you keep the eco-graffiti alive for? Try painting on different surfaces such as brick and wood. Which surface is best for growing eco-graffiti?

MEASURE WIND SPEED WITH AN ANEMOMETER

Some days there is hardly any wind at all, whilst other days the wind is so strong it feels like it could blow you off your feet. Build a device to measure wind speed, called an anemometer, then see how it changes from day to day.

Using the hole punch, make two holes opposite each other just below the rim of one of the paper cups. Push one of the straws through these holes so it sticks out on either side.

Now turn the cup through 90 degrees and do the same thing again. The cup should now have two straws poking through it, and they should cross in the middle. This is the base.

Calculate the wind speed. Hold the anemometer out of a car window whilst being driven along at 10mph (16km/h). Count the number of rotations in 30 seconds. If you count five rotations, you know that five rotations equals 10mph (16km/h). This is your benchmark. When you use the anemometer later you'll know, for example, that ten rotations in 30 seconds means a wind speed of 20mph (32km/h).

Take another paper cup. Using the hole punch, make two adjacent holes halfway down the cup. The holes should be roughly 2cm (3/4in) apart. Do the same for the remaining three cups. These are the sails.

Now take these sails, one at a time, and push them onto the straws sticking out from the base. Guide the straws through the holes in the sails so they just poke out the other side. The sails should all be facing in the same direction.

Use the tip of a sharp pencil to poke a hole in the bottom of the base. The hole should be in the centre of the base and it should be big enough to poke a pencil through. Now push the blunt end of the pencil through the hole so the rubber rests underneath the place where the two straws cross.

Holding the pencil for support, lightly push the drawing pin through the two straws and into the rubber. Be gentle! If you press it in too hard, the anemometer won't work. Try giving the anemometer a spin. If it rotates freely, it's good to go.

Stand outside on a windy day and count how many times the anemometer spins in 30 seconds.

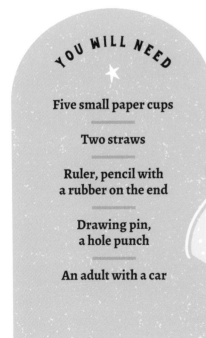

YOU WILL NEED

Five small paper cups

Two straws

Ruler, pencil with a rubber on the end

Drawing pin, a hole punch

An adult with a car

MAKE A ROSE PETAL
BATH BOMB

**Lie back and relax with some homemade bath bombs
scented with ingredients from the garden. Which flowers
give the most satisfying scent?**

YOU WILL NEED

300g (10¹/₂oz)
bicarbonate of soda

150g (5oz) cream of tartar

Two teaspoons olive oil

Large mixing bowl

Essential oils (any you like)

Wooden spoon

Food colouring

Handful of rose petals

Water in a spray bottle

Silicon ice-cube tray

Add the bicarbonate of soda,
cream of tartar and olive oil to a
large mixing bowl. The olive oil
helps to bind the ingredients
together and will moisturise your
skin in the bath. Add a few drops
of essential oil. Any will do, but
lavender oil works really well.

Use a wooden spoon to mix all
of the ingredients together. Add a
few drops of food colouring. Do not
add the whole bottle. You probably
don't want to end up with blue or
pink or green skin.

At this stage the mixture will still
be powdery. This is to be expected.
Tear up the rose petals into small
pieces and add them to the mix.
Give it another stir, then add a few
sprays of water. Listen carefully.

What do you hear? The mixture should begin to fizz as the ingredients start to react.

Keep stirring the mixture until it becomes the texture of wet sand. Don't add too much water or all the fizz will disappear and there will be none left for the bath.

Take small handful-sized blobs of the mixture and press them into the silicon ice-cube mould. The mould will help to stop the bombs from crumbling. Take care not to touch your eyes at this point, because the mixture could irritate them.

Rose petals have a beautiful scent, but what other plants can you find that have soothing aromas? Try making bath bombs with crushed lavender seeds or grated orange peel.

Now for the difficult part. Leave the bombs to set. This will take one to two days. Make sure they are totally dry and hard before removing them from the mould. Add them to a bath full of warm water, step in and relax.

TORNADO
IN A BOTTLE

When they occur naturally, tornadoes can destroy trees, houses and cars. Make a mini tornado in a bottle. It won't destroy anything (I promise) but it will help to explain how real tornadoes form.

YOU WILL NEED

Two equal-sized plastic bottles with lids

Scissors

Food colouring

Duct tape

Remove the lid from one of the bottles. Using the scissors, cut a neat, circular hole in the middle of the lid. The hole should be about 1cm (½in) across. This is fiddly, so you may need an adult's help. Now make an identical hole in the lid of the second bottle.

Add a couple of drops of food colouring to one of the empty bottles then top it up with water. The water should almost reach the top of the bottle. Swirl the bottle around to make sure the food colouring and water mix together. The colouring makes it easier to see the tornado.

Screw the lids back on to both of the bottles as tightly as you can. Place the empty bottle upside down on top of the bottle that contains the water. Tightly wrap lots of duct tape around the lids. In a moment you're going to turn it all upside down and you don't want the water leaking out. This step is also fiddly, so you may need to bother an adult again.

*Real tornadoes form
in a similar way. They occur
when a downward current
of air from a thundercloud
sucks in air from its
surroundings, creating
a rapidly spinning
column of air.*

Carefully turn the device upside down and stand it on a table. What happens? The bottom bottle may look empty but it's actually full of air. The water in the top bottle is pressing down on the air, but the air in the bottom bottle is pushing back against the water. This keeps the water in the top bottle.

Pick up the bottles and swirl them around in a circular motion. Now what happens? The movement allows air to escape upwards into the top bottle. This creates a column of spinning water that is wider at the top and narrower at the bottom. This is your tornado. The water will now start to pour through the connection. Time how long the water takes to flow into the bottom bottle.

MAKE MUSHROOM PRINTS

Mushrooms aren't plants or animals. They are fungi. Try making beautiful mushroom prints with the fungi from your fridge.

Collect some mushrooms. Some wild-grown mushrooms can be poisonous if they are eaten, so it's best to use shop-bought mushrooms for this experiment. You're not going to eat them, but it's good to be safe. The mushrooms need to be fresh and juicy, not old and dried out.

The mushrooms that we see in the supermarket are the bit of the fungus that grows above ground. Let's start by learning about the mushroom's structure. Draw a picture of a mushroom in your science journal. Label the stem, which is the bottom part, and the cap, which is the top part. Look underneath the cap. Can you see lots of tiny folds? These are called gills, but they're not like the gills

YOU WILL NEED
★

Mushrooms

Knife

Black and white paper

Large pebbles

Bowl

that fish have. Mushroom gills contain tiny seed-like structures called spores. When the spores are released from the cap of the mushroom, they can germinate and produce new fungi. Label the gills on your diagram.

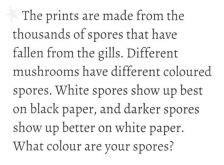

It's time to make the print. Take two mushrooms that are the same. Cut off their stems and discard them. Place one cap on a piece of white paper, and the other on a piece of black paper. The gills should be facing down. Place a large pebble on each mushroom. The pebble should be big enough to weigh the mushroom down, but not so big that the mushroom is squashed.

Cover the mushrooms with a bowl to help prevent them from drying out. Leave the mushrooms overnight. In the morning, carefully remove the bowl, pebble and mushroom. How do your prints look?

DID YOU KNOW?
Fungi can't eat food like animals, and they can't make their own food like plants. Instead they absorb nutrients from nearby plant or animal matter.

The prints are made from the thousands of spores that have fallen from the gills. Different mushrooms have different coloured spores. White spores show up best on black paper, and darker spores show up better on white paper. What colour are your spores?

Repeat the experiment, this time with a different variety of mushroom. Supermarkets sell many different kinds of mushrooms including oyster, portobello and the more familiar white mushrooms. What do their spore prints look like? Remember that the prints contain live spores, so don't put these in your journal. Photograph your prints and stick the photos in your journal instead.

MAKE A CLOUD
IN A JAR

The closest that most of us get to clouds is when we fly through them in an aeroplane. Make a mini cloud in a jar and learn how clouds form.

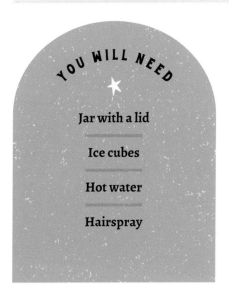

YOU WILL NEED

Jar with a lid

Ice cubes

Hot water

Hairspray

It is safest to do this experiment in the kitchen sink. Unscrew the lid from the jar and turn it upside down. Place three or four ice cubes inside the upturned lid. Ask an adult to help you half-fill the glass jar with freshly boiled water, then balance the upturned lid on top of the jar. Watch the jar for 5 minutes. What happens?

Empty the jar and repeat the experiment. Half-fill the jar with freshly boiled water but this time, add a good squirt of hairspray into the jar before placing the cold lid on top. Watch for 5 minutes. What do you see this time?

Water evaporates from our oceans, lakes and rivers, and rises up into the air as water vapour. As the water vapour gets higher, the air gets cooler. This makes the water vapour condense into tiny droplets of water. When droplets join together they become heavier and fall as rain.

In the first experiment you probably saw tiny drops of water form on the sides of the jar. The warm water vapour rose up inside the glass and condensed into droplets when it touched the cold lid.

For clouds to form, something else needs to happen. The tiny droplets of water vapour in the sky need to meet and mix with tiny particles of dust, ice or sea salt. The droplets and the particles stick together and this makes a cloud.

There were no dust particles in the first experiment, but in the second experiment, the hairspray acted like dust. Tiny water droplets stuck to particles of hairspray. This made the cloud in the jar.

Now for the fun part. It's time to set your cloud free. Carefully remove the lid and watch the cloud disappear. If you've ever wanted to touch a cloud, now's your chance!

See if you can make better clouds by squirting other harmless aerosols into the jam jar. Can you make clouds with deodorant or air freshener?

DID YOU KNOW?
Other planets have clouds, too, but they're not made of water. Jupiter has clouds that contain molecules made of ammonia and sulphur.

PREDICT THE WEATHER

Weather forecasters predict the weather using a device called a barometer. Make your own barometer and see if your weather predictions are better than the professional ones.

Balloon, rubber band

Scissors

Glass jar

Coloured tape

Paper straw

Piece of A4 card

Ruler, pen

Our planet is surrounded by a layer of air that is nearly 100km (60 miles) thick. This is called the atmosphere. The atmosphere presses down on Earth creating atmospheric pressure. As the air warms and cools, and picks up or loses water, the atmospheric pressure changes. You can detect these changes with your barometer.

Cut the neck off the balloon and throw it away. Stretch the main part of the balloon over the opening of the jar. Pull it tight to get rid of any bumps or creases, then secure it in place using a rubber band. The air inside the jar is now unable to escape.

Put a small piece of tape over one end of the straw. Use the tape to attach the straw to the middle of the stretched-out balloon. The straw should now be horizontal and sticking out at right angles to the jar.

As the atmospheric pressure changes and air presses down on the balloon more or less, the straw will move up and down. To see how much movement there is, you need to make a scale.

To make the scale, fold the piece of A4 card in half lengthways. Using a ruler, draw horizontal lines spaced 1cm (½in) apart down one side of the card. On the top half of the card draw a sun. On the bottom half draw a cloud.

Set up your barometer indoors, in a place where the temperature doesn't change much. Don't put it near a window or a radiator, as this will make the air inside the jar expand or contract, and affect the readings. Place the scale next to the jar so the straw is pointing at one of the lines.

Take readings every day. Does the dial move up or down? Make a note of your readings. How do they compare with the local weather forecast?

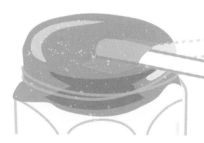

When the atmospheric pressure is low, there is less pressure pushing down on the balloon and the dial points down. This means that rain is coming. When the atmospheric pressure is high, there is more pushing down on the balloon and the dial will point up. This means it will be dry and sunny.

BUILD A THERMOMETER

Traditional thermometers measure the temperature using a liquid metal called mercury, but you can make your own thermometer using just the water from the tap. Make a record of the daily temperature.

Fill the bottle with water almost to the top, and add a few drops of food colouring. Swirl the bottle around so the food colouring mixes with the water.

Measure down 5cm (2in) from the top of the straw and make a mark. Measure down 10cm (4in) from the top of the straw and make a second mark. Roll a big lump of modelling clay or plasticine into a fat sausage and wrap it around the straw to make a doughnut shape. Adjust the doughnut so the top of the ring is level with the second mark.

Place the straw into the bottle. Make sure the bottom of the straw doesn't touch the bottom of the bottle. The doughnut will make a lid and prevent the straw from falling into the water. Mix up a little more water and food dye, then use the pipette to drip some of the mixture into the straw. The aim is to raise the water level so that it reaches the top mark.

Add two drops of oil to the straw. Oil and water are immiscible. This means they don't mix, so the oil will form a layer on top of the water. This will stop the water from evaporating.

⭐ Your thermometer is ready to use. Stand it in a bowl of icy water. What happens to the water level? Mark the new water level with a pen. The temperature of icy water is 0°C (32°F) so this new mark also corresponds to 0°C (32°F). Write a '0' (or '32') next to the mark.

Try measuring other things. What's the temperature outside? How about your bath water? Is it closer to 100°C (212°F) or closer to 0°C (32°F)?

⭐ Now stand the thermometer in a bowl of water that has just boiled. (Ask an adult to help you with this.) What happens to the water level now? This second new mark corresponds to the temperature of boiling water: 100°C (212°F). Write '100' (or '212') next to the mark.

WRITE WITH INVISIBLE INK

You don't have to be a spy to write in invisible ink. Learn how to create and decipher secret spy messages using just lemons and a candle.

Cut the lemon in half and squeeze all of the lemon juice into a bowl. Remove any pips that fall into the mixture. Add a couple of teaspoons of water and stir it well. The secret ink is ready to use.

DID YOU KNOW?
During the Second World War, prisoners of war wrote messages in invisible ink. They didn't have lemons or orange juice, so they wrote their secret messages in urine, which is also weakly acidic.

Dip your paintbrush into the ink and write your secret message on a piece of paper. Work quickly because as the ink dries, it becomes impossible to see. If you have an old-fashioned calligraphy pen, you can dip the nib in the ink and write with that. Allow the paper to dry.

Ask an adult to decipher the secret message. Get them to light a candle and hold the paper above the flame. Don't hold it too close or the message will go up in flames! Move the paper around over the heat source. What do you see? The message will be revealed.

This invisible ink works because the acidic lemon juice browns more quickly than the rest of the paper. What else could you use to make invisible ink? Try making invisible ink from other acids, like vinegar, apple juice and orange juice. Which works the best? Can you think of any other ways to reveal the secret message?

Heat is the key. Place the paper on a radiator or ask an adult to iron the paper for you. Both methods should work. Another way to read the message is to put salt on the drying ink. Leave the salt for one minute then wipe it away. When you want to display the message, colour over it with a wax crayon and the message will appear.

YOU WILL NEED ★

A lemon

Knife

Bowl, water

Fine paintbrush

Paper

Candle, matches

BUILD A MINI RAFT

This is a great activity for a rainy day. Build a mini raft then test it in the kitchen sink. How many coins can it hold before it capsizes?

Collect at least five long, straight sticks. Break off any side branches that are poking out and then snap the sticks so they are all roughly the same length. Your raft needs to be able to fit comfortably in the kitchen sink, so don't make the sticks too long or too big.

YOU WILL NEED

Straight sticks

Kitchen sink

String

Four wooden ice lolly sticks

Glue

Coins

Lay the sticks out next to one another to form the base of the raft. Tie the sticks together using the string. The best way to do this is to tie the string around one end of the first stick and make a knot. Then loop the string around the end of the next stick and make a knot. Then loop the string around the end of the next stick . . . and so on, until you reach the last stick. Make a final knot to keep the last stick secure.

Now do the same for the other end of the raft. Secure the sticks by tying the ends together with string.

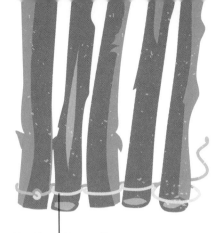

Knotting the raft

Lay two ice lolly sticks on top of the string and glue them in place. Now turn the raft over and do the same on the other side. This will give the raft extra stability. Allow the glue to dry thoroughly.

Fill the sink with water and lower your raft in. Does it float or sink? Guess how many coins your raft will be able to hold before it capsizes. Write your prediction down in your science journal. Now add the coins one at a time. Were you right?

How can you alter the raft to make it hold more coins? Can you make it bigger? Take a look in the kitchen cupboards and around the garden. Is there anything you can add to make it more buoyant? Now repeat the coin test. Did you manage to improve your raft?

Balance coins on top

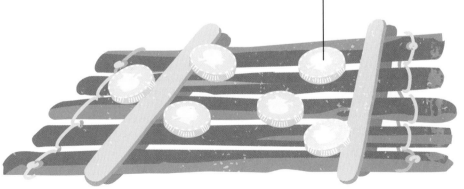

DIY FOSSILS

Why wait millions of years for fossils to form when you can make your own fossils today? Follow this recipe and make fossil imprints from the living things you find around you.

YOU WILL NEED

★

Mixing bowl and spoon

100g (3¹/₂oz) plain flour

100g (3¹/₂oz) table salt

175ml (6fl oz) water

Rolling pin

Biscuit cutters or a glass

Items from the garden, such as leaves and pine cones

Fossils are the remains of prehistoric life forms that lived millions of years ago. Sometimes plants and animals become fossilised, but sometimes their footprints or outlines become etched into stone. These are called trace fossils and they're very important because geologists can learn a lot from them.

To make some modern trace fossils, first prepare the dough. Add the flour and salt to the mixing bowl, and give it a stir with a spoon. Add the water, a little at a time, mixing as you go. The mixture should become doughy. When it's ready, it should come away from the side of the bowl cleanly.

Sprinkle a little flour on a work surface. Scoop up the dough with your hands and shape it into a ball on the powdered surface. Roll the mixture flat until it forms a layer around 2cm (3/4in) thick. Cut out circles using a biscuit cutter or an inverted glass.

Choose an item for your first trace fossil. Flowers and leaves leave beautiful imprints, as do pine cones and empty snail shells. Gently press the item into the dough. It shouldn't disappear completely but it should sink slightly into the dough. Press down on all of the features to make a good imprint.

Carefully remove the item from the dough using your fingers. What do you see? There should be a detailed impression of the item left in the dough. Place the dough somewhere warm where it can dry overnight, like an airing cupboard or a windowsill.

Look up some photos of fossilised plants, seeds and shells on the internet like the picture above. Evolution causes living things to change over time. How similar or different are your fossils to ones from the distant past?

DID YOU KNOW?
Trace fossils include
footprints left by prehistoric
animals, but they also
include other items that
animals leave behind.
These can include nests,
burrows and even
dinosaur poo!

WASH WITH CONKER SOAP

Conkers are the seeds of the horse chestnut tree. They contain soapy chemicals called saponins. Make some conker soap and then see how well it works.

YOU WILL NEED

About thirty fresh conkers

Sharp knife, scissors

Cheese grater

Large bowl, water

Muslin cloth

Small plastic container

Old piece of fabric

Regular bar of soap

Peel the skin from the freshly fallen conkers using a sharp knife. Conkers are quite small so this can be fiddly. You may want to ask an adult for help. Grate the conkers into tiny pieces using the cheese grater. This is even more fiddly. You'll almost certainly want to ask an adult for help. To avoid grating your fingers, hold each conker firmly and grate them slowly.

Fill the bowl up with warm tap water and drape the muslin cloth over the top. Press the muslin cloth into the water so the middle part is submerged and the edges are hanging over the sides of the bowl.

Collect all the conker gratings and place them in the middle of the bowl inside the muslin cloth. Leave the

mixture to soak for a couple of hours, then gather the edges of the cloth into a bundle and remove it from the water. The conker pieces should still be inside the muslin.

Squeeze the muslin to remove the excess water. Keep squeezing until the mixture inside the cloth

forms a tight, compact lump. Open the cloth up and squidge handfuls of the mixture into the plastic container. Leave the soap to dry in a warm, dry space overnight, then turn it out of the container.

It's time to test the conker soap. Take the old piece of fabric out in the garden and kick it around in the dirt. Make it as messy and dirty as possible, then cut it in half to make two equally dirty, smaller pieces of cloth.

Fill the sink with warm water. Scrub one piece of cloth with regular soap, and another with conker soap. Which cleans the best?

KEEP EXPERIMENTING!

So, did the experiments work? What have you learned? What was the best, the messiest and the most unexpected finding? What worked well? What didn't go so well?

★ The great thing about experiments like these is that there are always more things you can try. In science, one question always leads to another. So if, for example, you dyed a T-shirt with the natural avocado dye (pages 154–55) and it turned out very pale, what could you do to make the colour stronger?

★ This book may almost be finished, but the experiments don't have to be. Plan some more experiments of your own. Start by asking a question, like the one above, and then use that question to make a hypothesis. A hypothesis is just a sentence that describes what you think is likely to happen. For the avocado experiment, a new hypothesis could be: Adding stones and skins to the mix will make the colour stronger.

DID YOU KNOW?
More than 500 years ago, people were writing with avocado ink. Some of the ruby-coloured documents exist to this day.

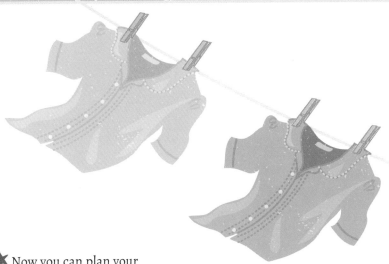

★ Now you can plan your experiment. Good experiments always have an 'experimental' and a 'control' group. The control group is the part of the experiment where nothing changes. This gives you a benchmark against which to measure any changes that you make. The experimental group is the part of the experiment where you test new things.

★ So, dye one T-shirt using the original recipe (with stones only). This is the control group. And dye another T-shirt using your new recipe (with stones and skins). This is the experimental group. Then compare the results. Was your hypothesis correct? If the T-shirt in the experimental group was darker than the T-shirt in the control group, then your hypothesis was correct.

★ Now whatever you do, please don't restrict yourself to the experiments in this book. Ask questions, make hypotheses and design experiments about the world around you. Find out things that no one else knows, and if your hypothesis turns out to be wrong, don't worry. Scientists do sometimes find that their hypotheses are wrong and this is how some of the most exciting breakthroughs in science are made. Scientists are continually revising what they know about the world as they perform more and more experiments to test their hypotheses. Be curious, be inventive and be bold, but most of all, enjoy your garden science.

CREDITS

AUTHOR'S ACKNOWLEDGEMENTS

Thanks to Kate Duffy, Lindsey Johns and Sarah Skeate for their brilliant editorial and artistic skills. And thanks to my family and my dog. For being there.

PICTURE CREDITS

The publishers would like to thank the copyright owners for permission to reproduce their images. Every attempt has been made to obtain permission for use of the images from the copyright holders. However, if any errors or omissions have inadvertently occurred the publishers will endeavour to correct these for future editions.

Alamy Stock Photos: Anne Elizabeth Mitchell 23; A D Fletcher 27; blickwinkel 57; daisyforster 97; dalekhelen 41; Dorling Kindersley Ltd 29, 43, 83; Linda Kennedy 49; Minden Pictures 89; Roger Parkes 53; George Philip 61; Adrian Sherratt 161; Dani Simmonds 99.

Carly Schmitt 167.

Getty Images/The Image Bank/Jeffrey Coolidge 109.

iStock: 13; 103.

Science Photo Library /Steve Gschmeissner 67T.

Shutterstock: 6, 7, 10, 11, 35, 45, 54, 67BR, 71, 88–89, 92, 93, 103, 107, 119, 125, 129, 137, 143, 144, 145, 148, 149, 163, 171, 175, 187, 189, 190.

Wikipedia Onderwijsgek at nl.wikipedia 66.